Leadership Within the School Library and Beyond

By Lesley S. J. Farmer

Linworth Publishing, Inc.
Worthington, Ohio

Library of Congress Cataloging-in-Publication Data

Farmer, Lesley S. J.
  Leadership within the school library & beyond / by Lesley S.J.
Farmer
          p.   cm. -- (Professional growth series)
  Includes bibliographical references.
  ISBN 0-938865-40-4 (paperback)
  1. School libraries--United States--Administration.
2. Leadership. I. Title. II. Series.
Z675.S3F237   1994
0.25.1'978--dc20

                                                                                94-45621
                                                                                    CIP

Published by Linworth Publishing, Inc.
480 East Wilson Bridge Road, Suite L
Worthington, Ohio   43085

Copyright © 1995 by Linworth Publishing, Inc.

Series Information:

        From The Professional Growth Series

ISBN 0-938865-40-4

5 4 3 2 1

Table of Contents

Section 7: Leadership Within the School: The Second Ring of Power

Section 8: Leadership Within the Community: The Third Ring of Power

Section 9: Leading Within the Profession: The Fourth Ring of Power

Section 10: The Audience Role of Following

Bibliography

Acknowledgements

About the Author

Lesley S.J. Farmer is a Library Media Teacher at Redwood High School in Larkspur, California. She has extensive experience as a school librarian, as a young adult and children's specialist in public libraries, and as a library science instructor, most recently at San Jose State University. Dr. Farmer is the author of a number of articles and books on librarianship.

Linworth Publishing, Inc. would like to thank the following school librarians and teachers for their contributions to *Leadership Within the School Library and Beyond*:

Shirley Fetherolf, Lakewood High School, Lakewood, Ohio
Diane Pozar, Wallkill Middle School, Wallkill, New York

Section 1
Rings of Influence

Once upon a time there was an eager, bright-eyed school librarian who dreamed of a special media center of her very own. It would be filled with the most exciting books and audiovisuals. There'd be nooks for students to crawl in and read escape novels. There'd be state-of-the-art computers with students, boys and girls, swarming around and teaching each other the delights of Boolean searching. Competent and caring staff, both volunteer and paid, would complement the school librarian's activities.

And the teachers: they'd be incorporating literacy skills across the curriculum, planning and team-teaching lessons—nay, whole units and culminating learning experiences—with the school librarian. The library would be the heart and brain of the school, recognized and totally supported by the administration and school community. Why, the school media center would have its name in lights—and appear in the American Library Association's video on exemplary media programs.

The dewy-eyed school librarian searched a year and a day for just the perfect library, but none was exactly right. One had musty old books, another had musty old teachers, and one had no students using the library at all! It was very frustrating.

Just when she thought she would never succeed, a kind, wise woman appeared. "Dear, the answer isn't in the library. The answer is in you. *You must become a school librarian* leader." *The woman vanished as quickly as she had appeared, leaving the school librarian alone with her thoughts.*

"She's right! My quest has just begun," she said to herself. And with that, the renewed school librarian advanced confidently, knowing that somehow she would reach her goal—and her library.

Yes, she can make her dream library come true. And so can the rest of us, at least those of us who are willing to join in the quest of becoming school librarian leaders.

As I pursued an administrative credential, with dreams of becoming a district librarian, I saw the critical need for a book on school librarian leadership. Why? Because school media centers have changed from warehouses to information and curricular centers. And school librarians have changed from clerks to educational partners. The next step upward is to educational leader, the role emphasized in *Information Power*, (published by the American Association of School Librarians and the American Library Association), as necessary to implement the mission of school library programs: "Leadership is the crucial factor in creating a quality library media program that is an integral part of the school curriculum." (AASL, p. 42)

One of the symbols of educational leadership is "The Piece of Paper," so I pursued the continuing education route to enhance my leadership opportunities. Here I was, the only school librarian in the educational administration program. And there had not been many before me, even though California school librarians need that credential for an administrative position. Really, aren't all school librarians administrators, directing effective programs by managing the needed resources, material and human? And as administrators, shouldn't we be leaders? How else will we garner the resources and authority to carry out our mission effectively?

Too many of us feel thwarted by lack of those needed resources and authority. Maybe we get no support from administrators. Maybe budget cuts wound us deeply. Maybe the school or community atmosphere is stifling or apathetic. We don't feel in control of the situation.

Yet we *do* possess some control, at least of ourselves and our reactions to the world around us. What can we accomplish, given this unfriendly environment? Can we change that environment? Can we operate in another environment?

I can absolutely guarantee that even in the most limited, negative school environment you can become a leader if you want to be, if for no other reason than that our profession is bigger than any one place or any one function.

On the most global level, librarian leaders are desperately needed. With the societal crises of illiteracy, poverty, alienation, and socio-economic divisions, librarians are "ecologists of the mind," as Theodore Roszak asserts. We ensure equitable access to ageless minds' insights into life's concerns. Particularly because schools help form young minds, school librarians are in a critical position to positively influence society.

To me, these challenges became the call for a book on school librarianship. If I answered the call, what would I say? I thought about rings of influence: ourselves, our school libraries, our schools, our communities, our profession. A pebble dropped into a pond causes ripples across the water—rings of influence. The image worked.

That rippling effect can cause a tidal wave. School, frequently, is not a friendly environment for people who rock the boat, who cause too many ripples. Each school media center has its own norms and values, which need to harmonize with the school's culture in order to function effectively. In my administration courses I noticed that the concept of school "culture" was underrated. That needed to be addressed in a book on librarian leadership.

Then I started thinking about "empowerment": how school librarians can feel empowered, how they can empower faculty and students to lifelong learning. Visions of human development and information power came to mind. My book was taking on a personal approach.

The next breakthrough had to do with "the vision thing" in general. Schools, and other organizations, increasingly emphasize the need for a vision or mission to guide all thinking and action. Business has embraced TQM, Total Quality Management, as a means of looking at the total working environment to improve production and morale. The image of a beacon has been used repeatedly. Other images came to mind: the guiding star, the light at the end of the tunnel, the dream, the corporate symbol. I started thinking about the vision quest, about "naming" the process of leadership through envisioned images. Could I invoke stimulating images throughout the text?

As I researched the field, I came across an increasing emphasis on tranformational leadership: the leader as a change agent for personal development. Leadership roles can be shared; one person doesn't have to have all the power all of the time. This approach also melded into discussion about gender roles and leadership styles.

Looking at these elements, I also reflected on the school librarian's functions. One that seemed particularly vital for elementary school librarians was storytelling. In traditional societies, the storyteller or shaman had a vision and shared that revelation with the others. With the concept of the leader as a person apart, with a vision, who leads others to realize that vision, the parallels of storyteller and leader became obvious.

But it was a radio show about Xerox lore that clinched it for me. We have all seen those office cartoons that circulate across fax wires: the guy being skewered; the secretary saying, "You want it WHEN???" These and many other similar memos have become office lore, reflecting an organization's culture. This pop culture link with folklore, along with the storyteller function as visionary, led me to the conviction that the fairy tale, fable, or folktale could serve as a metaphor for school librarian leadership.

In fairy tales, the hero comes to an awareness of his inner resources so he can successfully battle ogres or dragons. Folktales do not tell the reader what to do, but they can act as a therapeutic mirror. Readers can find their own solutions by contemplating what the story means with relationship to their own inner conflicts at the time (Bettelheim, p. 25). By reflecting on folktales, participants can use their integrated, perhaps unconscious, knowledge in their everyday worlds.

For example, one of the most significant tasks in leadership is the task of socialization, how to get along with people and move them. Those rules of social contact are codified and passed down through the generations. In the school, it's called "tradition." Just as folktales such as *Snow White* and *King Thrushbeard* serve to teach those codes of conduct, school traditions and ritualized observances codify school values.

Beyond a local setting, folktales depict general human behavior in an international language of abstract, stereotyped situations. And yet folktales present living realities. A folktale can show evil, or obstacles, in concrete form. Characters in the story examine those barriers objectively so that they can be set inwardly free from them and overcome them. In the folktale, evil—and humans—can be radically transformed into good (Grahl, pp. 14, 32). It is this message of solid hope that empowers the persons absorbing a folktale, and it can empower the school librarian to become a leader.

So I have chosen this folktale paradigm to bring focus to school librarian leadership. (Note that "folktale" here encompasses the broad field of fables, fairy tales, and parables as well as traditional folktales.)

The first section of the book deals with leadership characteristics: the archetype. The second section deals with the folkloric personal quest: the inner dreams and visions of the leader. The third section concentrates on organizational factors: the cultural lore that folktales transmit. The fourth section deals with power and empowerment: the magician and apprentice.

Then, just as the storyteller conveys the message of the quest and the folktale to transform society, so do the next four sections show how you, the school librarian, can be a leader, or a hero, developing rings of power within your library, your school, your community, and your profession.

The tenth section ties leadership with folklore from the follower's, or listener's, viewpoint. A bibliography concludes the volume.

Come with me as companion seekers on this quest for leadership. Librarians often feel isolated. But know that you are not alone. With this book, you have the moral support and experiential advice to help you become the leader that you are meant to be.

Section 2
Archetypes of Leadership

Lead, follow or get out of the way.

Plaque on Ted Turner's desk

Know your job, set a good example for the people under you and put results over politics. That's all the charisma you'll really need to succeed.

Dyan Macham

Envision ideal school librarian leaders. What would they look like? Professional. Well-groomed and well-dressed. Comfortable. Natural. Relaxed. An air of well-being and self-assuredness. They walk with confidence. They are outgoing and caring.

What would their library look like? Alive and full of people! The heart and intellectual center of the campus. Warm and inviting. Comfortable. Unique. Filled with a sense of a community learning actively, people working together and individually, using print and nonprint sources with confidence.

What would these librarians do? Provide the best library service, always searching for ways to make it better. Manage, instruct, inspire. Spend time with others planning, implementing, and evaluating. Work effectively with compassion and insight, inspiring others by modeling earnest commitment. Supervise fairly, and develop their volunteer and paid staff. Network widely with the entire school constituency, community, and profession. Lead a balanced life.

How would other people respond to them? With enthusiasm and respect. At ease, yet challenged to better themselves. Eager to work as partners with others.

As you envisioned the ideal school librarian leader, perhaps you thought of a colleague who exemplifies leadership characteristics. Maybe you remembered inspiring articles about effective media centers and the school librarians who make them happen. Did you see yourself in this role?

There's a leader in each one of us. The issue is how to make that leadership potential a reality.

Definitions
First, we need to define "leader" and "leadership." There are many operational definitions of these two terms:
- A leader is someone who makes a difference.
- A leader is someone who makes things happen.
- A leader is someone who asks the right questions.
- "A manager does things right, a leader does the right things." (Bennis and Nanus, p. 21)

- A leader walks the talk.
- "Leadership is a process in which individuals influence others toward achieving a goal." (Hellriegel, p. 419)
- "Leadership is the marshalling of skills possessed by a majority but used by a minority." (Bennis, p. 5)
- "Leadership over human beings is used when persons with certain motives and purposes mobilize, in competition or conflict with others, institutional, political, psychological, and other resources to arouse, engage and satisfy the motives of followers." (Burns, 1978, p. 1)

In folklore terms, the leader might be considered a hero: "The man or woman who has been able to battle past his personal and local historical limitations to the generally valid, normal forms. . . . His task and deed is to return then to us, transfigured, and teach the lesson he has learned of life renewed." (Campbell, p. 20) Thus, the leader-hero has to deal with his or her own demons, see the vision, and make that triumphant struggle a model for the community to follow. Interpreting the folklore image, someone once said that a leader is an individual who knows the way, goes the way, and shows the way.

Several issues arise from looking at these definitions:
- Leadership involves a *vision* or goal.
- Leadership is *people-based.*
- Leadership is a *process.*
- Leadership involves *accomplishment.*
- Leaders are persons who have the ability and power to carry out leadership tasks. They have a vision and a commitment to that vision. They can communicate that vision and motivate others to achieve it.

Archetypal Traits and Competencies

Folklore, while it tells specific stories within cultural contexts, concerns itself with universal truths and archetypes. So, too, while each leader is unique and works in unique situations, some common traits and competencies characterize effective leaders.

Interestingly, perceptions about the leader, or hero, have changed, particularly in the last 50 years. While the "scientific method" of management was touted in the '40s, the concepts of "change agent" and "corporate visionary" took over in the '60s and '70s. Now the emphasis is on decentralized team-focused action. In addition, changing demographics (such as increasing numbers of women and minorities and stiffer international competition) and advancing technology have further affected our present-day concept of leadership skills and attitudes.

The following areas of leadership represent current thinking:
- Management competence
- Technical competence
- Commitment
- Communication
- Monitoring and evaluation
- Creativity and innovation

Management

But isn't leadership what managers do? Craig Hickman's book title probably says it best: *Mind of a Manager, Soul of a Leader.* For really effective leadership, you need to be a good manager—plus. Most of the literature describes a manager as a person in authority who plans and uses resources (both human and material) wisely to carry out an organization's goals.

The critical factors distinguishing management and leadership are people and vision. Leadership depends on a *voluntary* relationship between people: those who want to lead and those who want to follow them. Managers are usually given "legitimate" authority; they don't have to win it (although they need to know how to use it). Second, the leader must have some sense of the future, of a potential. Managers can remain in the "now."

In fact, one way to see the difference between managers and leaders is to look at how they are evaluated. Managers are usually measured in terms of their *performance.* How well is their program running? Do they plan and implement efficiently? On the other hand, leaders are regarded in terms of *potential.* Do they have a focused vision with direction? Do they inspire and motivate? Do they instill confidence in a proactive environment? Management is necessary for stability, but leadership is called for in times of change, especially far-reaching transformation.

So what management skills do leaders need? A main component is *planning:* being able to set goals and develop strategies, provide and deploy the resources needed to accomplish those goals, implement and evaluate the plan, and modify it as necessary.

A related skill is *problem-solving:* analyzing a situation, gathering information, considering alternatives and consequences, and making reasoned decisions.

Organization is another managerial skill: the ability to put things and situations in order. Organization also relates to the efficient use of time and people.

Another important skill in managing is *communication.* In fact, an entire section in this book is dedicated to this skill. Basically, communication involves not only giving information in different modes, but also receiving information through active listening and critical analysis of messages sent.

Interpersonal skills are also necessary for the manager: establishing and maintaining good work relations, managing conflict, matching jobs with people, and developing staff.

Information Power gives specific examples of management duties of the school librarian:

- Developing, implementing, and communicating policies and procedures;
- Recording and reporting data;
- Operating the budget;
- Staffing;
- Organizing and directing the program; and
- Promoting and marketing the program. (AASL, p. 48-52)

These are the bedrock competencies that make the school media center "run good."

Technical Competence

Closely related to managerial competence is technical competence: knowing the field. A school librarian leader who doesn't know how to develop and maintain collections, who cannot do library research or instruct others in research techniques, who does not feel comfortable with a wide variety of informational media, quickly loses credibility with colleagues.

The school librarian leader must not only have a solid grounding in the theory and practice of library science, but must also keep abreast of its trends and developments.

Competent leaders also recognize their technical limitations and know how to access needed skills. Making sure that the best people are available not only makes technical sense but shows that the leader is self-confident enough to make good use of talent rather than be threatened by it.

Commitment

In order to be a credible leader, the school librarian has to be committed to a vision—and to the profession and the site which form the contexts of the vision.

That commitment must operate on two levels: the internal and the external. The leader must know intellectually and believe emotionally in the vision, in herself or himself, and in the possibility of making the vision a reality with the material and human resources available. That sense of commitment needs to be so integral to oneself that it seems to operate as an unconscious habit.

Of course, that commitment needs to be visible to the leader's colleagues. Do actions mirror beliefs? Does speech hark back to vision? As others experience a leader's commitment, walking the talk, they become aware of priorities. And as they accept and follow the leader's example, they feel more confident that their efforts will be supported.

Communication

Leadership necessitates open and honest communication. Associates need to know what the leader expects—and how to meet those expectations. Workers need to feel welcomed by their leader. They should be able to chat with him or her on a social level and know they will be listened to.

The effective leader communicates with a keen sense of
- Situation: at orientation, during times of change, at crisis points, and when new skills are required;
- Timing: when staff need it, when staff can accept it;
- Tone: professional, matching staff style, firm and fair, confidential.

It is not enough to be a "nice guy." The school librarian leader must share the vision—and the *way* to that vision—with associates and staff accurately, clearly, and in sufficient detail so that the goal will become a reality. Both quantitative skills and subjective values need to be articulated to ensure shared expectations. Such communication skill also entails giving timely corrective feedback and advice so that colleagues can get back on the right path if they waver or go astray.

Moreover, people need to feel comfortable enough to tell the school librarian if they think that he or she is off the track as well. The librarian needs to accept and reflect on such constructive criticism. Does the leader own the problem? Then the evidence is there on which to base the needed change. Even if a perception is inaccurate, the leader needs to know others' feelings in order to correct the perception.

Monitoring and Evaluation

The school librarian leader must pay attention to both the product and the process: the plan and the people. Like good car mechanics, school library leaders keep "tinkering" to maintain and improve whatever they drive. They don't subscribe to the "If it ain't broke, don't fix it" mentality; rather, they work on the theory that prevention is better than curative interventions.

One popular method of formative evaluation goes under the rubric of MBWA: Management by Walking Around. How does the library look? What are people doing in that environment? How is the library perceived throughout the school? Part of the process involves documenting and thinking about the manager's effectiveness as well; too often so much time is spent putting out brush fires and other immediate crises that important reflective time is sacrificed.

The ultimate concept is to keep one's eyes on the goal, see how well it's being attained, and decide if that goal is indeed the correct destination.

Creativity and Innovation

One aspect of leadership that is often overlooked is creativity and innovation, even though many settings manifest the limited results of limited imaginations. (And the even sadder situation where an uncreative "leader" feels threatened by creative workers who could benefit the organization.)

The creative leader sees more possibilities and more ways to reach them. The creative leader sees more obstacles and ways to surmount them. The creative leader makes existing material resources work beyond expectation and figures out how to generate new resources. The creative leader uncovers people's capabilities and thinks of ways to help them blossom. As creativity guru Roger van Oech explains, creativity involves the searching capabilities of the explorer, the formation skills of the artist, the evaluation insights of a judge, and the implementation practices of a warrior.

In brief, creativity enables the school librarian leader to be an effective agent for change, not only through looking ahead and planning for the future but also by anticipating and meeting people's needs in light of change. When creativity is employed for the good of the library, then librarianship becomes exciting, and the whole field is enriched.

Developing Leadership Skills

Fortunately, most leaders are made, not born. Conceptions about leadership have changed over time.

At one point, leadership was considered in terms of inherent traits. As with teaching, where some people have a natural tendency for instruction yet all can learn the science of teaching, leadership qualities begin to take form early in life but they can also be learned throughout life.

Particularly in the field of librarianship, that sense of lifelong learning is especially strong. Whether learning occurs in formal settings and results in degrees or certificates or happens during social hours at library conferences, whether ideas are shared in large groups or gleaned from the pages of a book, we school librarians who aspire to leadership need to keep mentally alert for opportunities to fine-tune our skills as leaders.

The following sections outline some of the skills that leaders employ and suggest ways to develop and practice these skills. The next section, however, goes to the heart of the issue: the internal values and attitudes of the school librarian. For it is the work we do within ourselves that manifests itself in meaningful leadership of others.

Section 3

The Quest for Personal Management

*The characteristic of a genuine hero is his persistency. All men
have wandering impulses, fits and starts of generosity. But
when you have resolved to be great, abide by yourself, and do
not weakly try to reconcile yourself with the world. The heroic
cannot be the common, nor the common the heroic.*

Ralph Waldo Emerson

At a recent conference I heard the brief but moving story of a new librarian.
He had been an engineer, but felt that something was missing. By happen-
stance he attended a library conference and was impressed with the vigor and
commitment of those around him. That serendipitous encounter led the
engineer to rethink his values and purposes, and he decided to attend library
school. At the next library conference he received a scholarship to pursue his
new career dream, and in accepting the honor, this ex-engineer challenged his
audience of librarians to keep their passion for librarianship as they continued
to make a difference in the world.

In folklore, the hero attains self-fulfillment and power only after he
follows—and returns from—a personal quest. Whether it's Hansel or Gretel
learning independence from the family or the contemporary Luke SkyWalker
who learns to use the Force wisely, folk heroes struggle against adversity to
understand and strengthen their own beliefs and strengths.

Likewise, we school librarian leaders must take time to reflect on and
strengthen our inner natures so we can lead others more effectively. For
personal values and actions lay the foundations for building credible, trusting
professional relationships and effective agendas.

Go to the Heart of the Matter

What beliefs do you consider important? What values do you demonstate in
your actions? They may not be one and the same. Are your values the same as
those of most leaders? These are questions you need to consider when looking
at yourself as a school librarian leader, for values are general guides to
behavior.

Values are derived from personal experience: teachings of authorities,
family traditions, cultural expectations, friends' influences, associations rising
out of personal interests, reactions to individual confrontations, responses to
physical characteristics. They arise out of repeated free choice and develop
throughout life.

Values clarification is a process by which one consciously looks at personal choices to discover what is important to oneself. By asking yourself what matters to you, you can determine which attitudes aid you as a leader and which attitudes you need to examine more closely so they will not trip you up in your work as a leader. As Don Koberg and Jim Bagnall assert in their book *Values Tech*:

> Although we may spend lots of time and energy trying to put
> together our beliefs, . . . it would be better to consider our
> beliefs as tentative things, things we are always trying on for
> size, not things which have such a permanent effect that we
> no longer need to watch out for how they might cramp our
> growth. (p. 134)

Here are some exercises to limber up your inner quester. Before you begin reading, get yourself prepared. Find a quiet spot, even if it's just mental, so you can "center" yourself. Have handy some kind of expressive tools: pen and paper, tape recorder, paints, computer. In this way, you can hold a dialogue with yourself. How often do you really contact your inner dragon and your best knightly friend, your inner being? As you read these mind conversation-starters, choose a couple that "connect" for you, and begin the interior quest. And remember that the right answer is the one that *feels* right to you—an authentic, real answer. Only as you open up to and confront yourself can you see what you have to give—to yourself and to others as a leader.

Personal timeline: On a blank sheet (or wall!) create a horizontal line, and label your birthday on the far left. Mark the line into decades of your life, and subdivide each decade into years. Plot significant points in your life: accomplishments, events, disappointments, relationships. Use the space above and below the line to designate your life's highs and lows. Start to ask yourself what patterns emerge—and why.

Pros and cons: List five things that you support the most, and five things you despise most. What commonalities occur within and between the two lists? What moves you the most? Why?

Good experiences: Whenever adversity hit me, my mother would say, "It's good experience, dear." Frankly, we do seem to learn more from our failures. Do you remember the answer you got right or the one you got wrong on a test? What were your greatest adversities or failures? How did you respond to them? What did you learn from them? Did they stem from outside or inner conflicts? How have adversities changed for you over the years, both in quantity and quality?

Good times: When we're in the midst of good times, we tend to feel better and act more positively. What are your good times? How do you like to spend your time? What makes you feel good? What friends make you feel good? When? What puts you in a good humor? Do these good elements tend to focus on one area of life, or do they represent different situations or approaches?

Masks: Librarians are often stereotyped, and as librarians we may show only parts of ourselves. What "mask" do you wear at work—to colleagues and to students? Is it the same mask? What other masks do you wear? To whom? When? Where? How do these masks differ from the authentic, unmasked you? Why do you wear these masks?

Countdown: Finish this line: "I am. . ." 10 times. Prioritize the statements in terms of their relative importance to you. Which ones of these "selves" could you live without being? If you could be only three of these, which would you choose? Why?

Obituary: Yes, the classic exercise: Write your own obit. How do you want to be remembered? What two statements would you want on your tombstone?

As you may have gathered, the most important aspect of these exercises is the interpretation of the inner data gathered. What patterns emerge, and why, begin to get at what makes you "tick" as a leader. As a reality check, you might want to enlist a confidante to see if her perceptions of you match your own beliefs. If they differ greatly, then that differential itself needs to be examined. Perhaps you need to educate others about who you really are.

Know What You Must Do

You have confronted your inner knights and dragons; now you can decide how to deal with them. As you compare your values to characteristics of leaders, you can begin to see whether you want to be a leader in the first place, and what areas need work if you want to improve your leadership potential.

Think of your personal quest as a means to develop a personal mission statement and strategies to accomplish that mission. Understand that you must determine what factors are under your control, and which are conditions you must accept (unless you can change your environment). Start by looking at your obituary—your final say about who you want to be; this is your mission in life. Then examine the list of "I am. . ." statements. Do they reflect who you want to be? If who you *are* is not what you want to *be*, then you are in personal conflict and must resolve that double-bind. Maybe you need to change your life's mission; maybe you need to raise your self-expectations.

Throughout life humans play out different roles relative to themselves and others. These roles may be categorized as follows:

- Self-service: physical maintenance (sleeping, eating, personal care);
- Professional: work that brings in money;
- Family: as parent, partner, child;
- Social-cultural-recreational: activities done with friends for enjoyment;
- Community: volunteer memberships (church, politics, social action); and
- Personal: activities usually done by yourself (leisure reading, TV).

Now identify activities that you *currently* do that relate to each role above, realizing that some activities overlap categories. Calculate the amount of time you spend at each, and add the hours within each role. You may want to develop a pie chart to visualize how your time is spent—and how you want to spend it.

Then in light of your "I am. . ." and mission statements, examine your time commitments and decide what you want to change within each role. Identify three or four objectives in each role area. Prioritize them in ABC fashion (A for high-value items, B for medium-value items, C for low-value items).

Now you are ready to put a time frame into your planning and implementation. Decide which goals are achievable within five years and which within one year. Then list specific strategies you can do within the next month and six months. By giving yourself a limited list of realistic "to do's" you are more apt to develop your leadership skills, as well as your whole personal life, in a systematic and achievable way. For good measure, give a good friend a copy of the list—and keep your own copy handy for frequent check-ups.

Since this process probably involves some self-changes, you need to help yourself succeed. Here are some "CRAFTy" tips to facilitate your self-management improvement:

- *Cancel* false negative images about yourself. You need to believe in yourself before you can expect others to believe in you. When you hear your negative inner voice, you may have to tell it to *stop* playing that old self-destructive tape.
- *Replace* negative images with successful, realistic images. Your subconscious needs to hear positive messages so it can get into the habit of feeling good.
- *Affirm* your self-image and personal goals to yourself and to others.
- *Focus* on your goals and immediate strategies to accomplish short-term objectives.
- *Train* yourself in new, successful roles. Take that needed workshop on budgeting. Exercise to regain your energy. Take time to go out with friends and renew your spirit. Learn those skills and practice them so you will be more successful as a librarian leader.

Be True to Yourself

You may have read self-improvement books about success that admonish one to take high risks, sell oneself enthusiastically, and Good Guy everyone. That approach may feel uncomfortable to you, like wearing sequins or blue jeans when you'd rather wear a three-piece suit or a dirndl.

As you look at your goals, you need to examine your own personality so you can achieve your personal mission according to your inner "rules." That same self-examination will also help you project your best self when dealing with others.

One popularized approach to classifying personality is the Myers-Briggs system. Books such as Keirsey and Bates' *Please Understand Me* (Prometheus Nemesis, 1978) and Kroeger and Thuessen's *Type Talk* (Delacorte, 1988) deal in depth with this analysis and provide practical tips on ways to work with people of differing personality styles. However, for the purposes of this book, a brief introduction to Myers-Briggs offers a glimpse into personality types and their application to personal management.

Basically, Myers-Briggs makes the assumption that people approach life in different ways. Using either-or statements, this system (which is largely based on Jungian theory) generates 16 personality archetypes. The categories are derived from responses to these questions:

- Where do you find your source of energy or direction: from within (Introversion), or in the company of others (Extroversion)?

- How do you take in information: from your senses, sequentially (Sensing), or from speculative hunches (iNtuition)?
- How do you come to conclusions: from your objective head (Thinking), or your subjective heart (Feeling)?
- What is your attitude towards the external world: task-oriented and resolved (Judging), or open-ended and flowing (Perceiving)?

The combination of categories loosely defines unique personality types. For instance, studies have found that school librarians are most likely to be ENFJ types. We tend to be extroverted (people-oriented), intuitive (future-oriented), feeling (sympathetic), and judging (goal-oriented). As such, we might experience frustration dealing with a go-with-the-flow, concrete-based, detached introvert. Knowing that personalities differ, the ENFJ school librarian, for example, could help ISTP individuals by giving them specific reasons for a decision and providing them sufficient time to get accustomed to that change by themselves.

Generally, as you get to know how your own personality works, you are better able to deal with people who are like—and unlike—you. You can be more tolerant, and can bring out the best in others to complement your strengths rather than compromising yourself.

Walk the Talk

No matter how positive your beliefs or how realistic your plans, if they are not put into action or perceived by others, then they won't do you any good. In fact, if what you believe does not jibe with what you do, others will be more likely to distrust you and you will be an ineffectual leader. If, however, you act authentically, then you will build a foundation of trust and credibility that will maximize both your potential as well as your colleagues'.

If you believe in mutual respect, you will promote equality, avoid doing "guilt trips," encourage independence, and participate as a partner. As a result, you and your colleagues will develop professionally and increase positive social behavior.

If you believe all people are important, including yourself, you will encourage input, refuse to be a "doormat," and know how to set limits. As a result, others will accept limits and know each other's rights.

If you believe that no one is perfect, but all can improve, then you will set realistic standards, encourage risk-taking, and focus on strengthening people. As a result, others will focus on task rather than self-protection and will have the courage to try new experiences.

If you believe in common professional values, then you will translate these values into informal norms that govern behavior, and you will promote collegiality. As a result, others will respond to professional norms, be more self-directed, and perform better.

As you look at your values and actions, give yourself progress reports.

- What do you notice about your behavior? Is it consistent with your mission? Do you feel comfortable with your actions? Do inner conflicts occur?
- How do others behave in response to you? Are you communicating your values so others are aware of them and understand where you

stand? Are you comfortable with your relationships?

- What inferences can be made about your values and actions in light of your observations? Are you in alignment with yourself and with others?
- What is your next course of action? Do you need to work on yourself or your connection with others?

A Last Note About Getting Along with Others and Yourself

Remember Benjamin Franklin's experiment in moral behavior? He listed his personal faults, and determined to correct them one by one. As he edged towards his goal, he realized that perfection could be hard to live with. It was better, he concluded, to have a few faults so others would be more amiable to him.

As you search within yourself, accept both the knight and the dragon aspects of your personality. Rather than denying or killing the dragon, harness it to make it work for you, providing the "fire in your belly" so the best, white-knight part of you can be a champion for school librarianship.

Section 4

The Folklore of the Organization

If you're going to sin, sin against God, not the bureaucracy.
God will forgive you but the bureaucracy won't.
                                                    Admiral Hyman G. Rickover

Library Media Teacher Susan set her daily schedule according to class periods. First period was planning time; just a few students came to the library then, usually to finish up homework, so Susan could get her first cup of coffee and look over papers. Second period she filed because she needed to show her presence; social studies teachers tended to bring in their classes. The teachers established a dependency relationship with their students, so the adult could act as savior; Susan acted as a guide for those students who either gave up waiting for the teacher or were too independent to hang on the teacher's words.

Third period? A bunch of "techies" used the library at that time, so Susan maintained a steady eye over those who would test the "system." Susan actually learned a few tricks from these guys and used her new skills to demonstrate that she could equal their interest in things electronic. Fourth period was Susan's dream period; her student aides were self-motivated and competent, so she could make those necessary phone calls and work on budget matters. It also geared her up for lunch , when the masses took over the library for socializing and Susan shelved as a way to supervise discreetly within arm's length of potential munchers.

So the periods continued until the moment Susan locked the library door and wrote down the user count for the day. Certainly each group had its own flavor; it was Susan's job to savor each bite.

Susan is one of those effective librarians who take the school organization as they find it, with its existing time schedule and class characteristics, and make it work for them. Not only are they aware of the social norms, but they enjoy working in harmony with those expectations, and they stretch those parameters in order to provide better service.

While the hero undergoes needed separation from the society in order to develop uniqueness and strength, he is not considered "redeemed" until he uses that newfound power to work within society and help reform it.

So, too, do we school librarian leaders need to recognize our schools' cultures in order to work effectively within them and be able to renew them. Library skills alone will not do the job. Even commitment to the library profession will not suffice. As librarians we need also to align ourselves with our organizational setting.

Too often we look at schools in terms of how they *ought* to operate rather than understand present practices so we can work effectively within the norms—and help change those norms to maximize learning. This chapter offers ways to see those realities and build a positive library climate within the organization.

Organizational Structure

What makes an organization? Two or more gathered in a work situation? People need to have some kind of structure (or even agree to have no structure) in order to know their roles, their connections, and their boundaries so they can carry out a group mission. There are several ways to look at structure, each of which reveals the school librarian's role within a work setting. Rather like an elephant being examined by blind men, organizational structure will be examined here from four perspectives. The composite view of these approaches should give a better idea of this complex "beast."

The organization as bureaucracy. An interesting operational definition of bureaucracy is "a place where it takes at least three telephone transfers to get to the person you want to talk to." Basically, a bureaucratic model deals with the following issues: hierarchy of authority, division of labor, rules and procedures, and impersonality. (Hellriegel, p. 319)

Let's look at a typical school situation. In an urban setting, Central High School demonstrates a strict, top-down hierarchy. The central administration makes all budgetary and operational decisions. A well-established department chair group decides curricular matters, under the strong supervision of the dean of faculty. Job descriptions are carefully delineated; each person has a specific and distinct duty and knows where he or she fits into the total picture. Rules and procedures are written for every situation. Mechanisms for dealing with infractions and appeals are also spelled out, so expectations are clear. The school treats everyone equitably, without regard to individual qualities.

In this environment the librarian needs to know the roles and rules throughout the school so he or she can operate smoothly within the organization. Clear expectations make it easier to work with students, and defined procedures help the librarian develop the collection in relation to the curriculum.

The organization as function. In this model, division of labor is based on task rather than titled position. The idea is to standardize activity, and group people doing similar work. Line activities in a school setting would refer to the teachers; staff activities would refer to service and support to faculty, such as the business office or personnel.

The school librarian can fall into either line or staff activity, depending on the school's philosophy. As a teacher partner, the librarian function can be structured as a line responsibility; however, as a cross-curricular administrator, the librarian might have greater affiliation with the dean of students or controller, and be considered a support staff person. Sometimes the librarian falls between the two groups, and has little say in school function at all. Ideally, the librarian should look at the school's functional divisions, see where the library can be the most effective, and then decide with which function to ally herself.

The organization as producer. In schools, the product is the student. In this model, people are organized according to defined "products" or programs. Thus, different disciplines work together to help a certain type of student. Competition may arise between groups, which is likely to increase within-group bonding and productivity. This type of structure lends itself especially to an outcome-based approach.

Let's examine Harvest Middle School, a suburban district site. A principal directs three grade-level "pods." Each pod is composed of four discipline-based teachers who team teach regularly; one acts as a team leader who facilitates the group's consensus-based decision-making. Students, too, have great say in how the school is run. In this environment, the librarian works collaboratively with the "pod" leaders and the principal. The library functions as a great "coming-together" place for the school, faculty and students alike.

The organization as matrix. This complex model takes into account the developmental stages of an organization. Basically, labor is divided along two dimensions: a permanent one such as grade-level or department, and a short-term one based on specific needs or problems. People thus report to two supervisors, depending on the situation. Particularly where schools are restructuring, this approach to organizational structure can be useful.

Chameleon Elementary School represents this model. Weekly planning sessions allow grade-level teachers to compare progress. Monthly staff meetings, however, focus on subject frameworks where representatives from each grade get together to develop articulated programs from K to 5. The librarian makes the rounds, visiting with a different grade level meeting weekly, and circulating among the framework groups each month. In this way, the librarian can know the entire curriculum and share ideas specific to each working group.

Knowing how an organization works, based on its structure, enables the librarian to maximize the library program's effectiveness to fit within the school's model of operation, whatever it is. While the trend in educational organizational structure is a "flatter," collaborative matrix or project model, any of the models above can be applied in examining how the library can operate best within the school.

Institutional Culture

It's one matter to understand an organization's structure; it's another to know how that structure plays out socially. This aspect speaks to the rich "folklore" of organizations.

Remember *Gulliver's Travels?* Talk about cross-cultural experiences! Gulliver continuously made faux pas and felt frustrated with each culture he encountered. And when he tried to bridge two cultures' approaches to cracking a egg, he was the one with egg on his face. Gulliver didn't understand or appreciate these cultural differences. Regardless of how he felt about each of them, Gulliver would have managed much better had he worked *with* each social norm rather than *against* it.

What exactly is meant by an organization's culture? In its broadest sense, *culture* can be defined as "the collective behavior patterns, communication styles, beliefs, concepts, values, institutions, standards, and other factors unique to a community that are socially transmitted to individuals and to which individuals are expected to conform." (Elster, p. 14) While people often associate culture with an ethnic or geographic group, a sense of culture prevails in most organizations.

The following exercise (adapted from Jan Elster, *Diversity: Creating Awareness and Avenues*) analyzes an organization's cultural traits. Entitled RUTSMAP, this tool can help you understand and appreciate an organization's uniqueness so you can work effectively within it. Keeping the organization in mind, respond to each set of questions:

- *Relationships:* How do people work together? As a team? In competition? Autonomously? What gender-linked roles exist?
- *Unions:* How do people socialize? In cliques based on fields of expertise or on personality? At school parties? In homes? What is the time frame for these social unions?
- *Teaching:* How do people learn? At in-services? Using mentors or buddies? Formally or informally? How is learning valued? What is the learning environment?
- *Spirituality:* What beliefs move the school community? What traditions are observed?
- *Medicine:* How does the organization measure its healthiness? What does it do when the group is in poor health?
- *Acquisitions:* How is money acquired and spent—on both human and material resources? Who makes the decisions? How much money is involved?
- *Politics:* What are the spoken and unspoken rules, and who develops and enforces them? How does the real power differ from the organizational chart?

As you look at your organization's RUTSMAP, what patterns arise? How can the RUTSMAP help you work within the organization? You may want to compare the organization's RUTSMAP with your personal RUTSMAP in order to discover possible areas of congruence or conflict.

Organizational culture involves norms of behavior: that is, a range of acceptable actions. The RUTSMAP reveals behavioral norms for your institution, though they may vary for specific situations and personalities. Those norms provide stability within the organization, and when someone behaves outside those norms, the behavior is usually met with subtle or overt disapproval. Norm conformity includes both performance standards and socialization. Norms can cause problems when group pressure results in lower productivity, or when excessive conformity stifles creativity or provokes rebellion. An additional challenge about norms is that they are often tacit; the newcomer may find it difficult to discover the organization's norms until he or she oversteps the boundaries. The school librarian needs to know the school's cultural norms in order to develop acceptable strategies for service and to suggest changes and improvements that will be acceptable. Within the library, the school librarian should set the norm for staff and student performance in order to establish clear expectations and appropriate behavior.

Cultural norms also speak to a third aspect of organizational culture: the individual's place in that group. Each person brings a unique set of skills and personal traits. Each one has a role to play. Each person relates to some degree with others in the group in terms of self-satisfaction and sense of belonging. As a leader, the librarian needs to keep the individual within the group in mind, so that all persons will want to give their best to the library because it's in their own best interests. The library will then act as a cohesive whole, greater than its parts.

Climate-Building

So how can you make use of organizational structure and climate as a librarian leader?

Library climate strongly determines how effective you can be as a librarian. And regardless of what you do, you automatically build a climate in the library, either positive or negative. So the best approach is to know what works to provide the desired outcome (your mission, your vision). As you analyze the school's culture, you can take the cues necessary to build on the good aspects and improve on the less effective aspects. With this start you can then observe what facilitates the learning environment you strive for: space allocation and traffic flow; supervision approaches; type of instruction; relationships with teachers, staff, and volunteers; and library materials and their promotion. The most important key is systematic planning: high awareness of the environment and ability to modify that environment efficiently.

While each setting is unique, some points about climate—building apply to most situations:

- *Make each person feel like a V.I.P.* Whether you use the hostess/ guest approach or partner perspective, make sure that your community feels Validated and encouraged, Informed, and Participative in their learning.
- *Act as a role model* to students and adults; let them know what you expect by acting it out yourself.
- *Be highly visible* in the library, the school, and the community. Attend school functions, visit classes, lunch with the faculty.
- *Involve students and faculty in short- and long-term planning.* Survey your constituents and follow through on their suggestions.
- *Focus on a few major issues* and check them closely. Examples might include team-teaching, student participation, technology integration, promotion of reading.
- *Assess the library regularly* to know where it stands relative to other areas of the school and to other libraries.
- *Include incentives* in the library program: a free treat to all library program participants, a party for library assistants, breakfast rolls for visiting faculty.
- *Use student and adult input* when developing and enforcing library rules and policies. Review these policies annually with constituents.
- *Help each student become successful in the library,* through a variety of instructional strategies and reinforcements.

- *Balance the collection* between curriculum and personal interest subjects, between books and periodicals and nonprint materials.
- *Involve parents and the community in the library* through volunteering, donations, events, public relations, and library access.
- *Promote team-building* through constituent representation in shared decision-making and implementation.
- *Balance the needs* of the institution and its administrators, staff needs, and individual needs by seeking overriding mutual goals and maintaining self-esteem.
- *Communicate positively, clearly, and accurately* with the total school community. Let them know that you are there for their benefit, as a valuable educational partner.

Rite On

In storytelling, rites assume a major role. Stories may be told just in a prescribed location, at a certain time, with people grouped in a particular way. There is often a specific way to open and close the session. These ritual actions each have meaning, and they give added meaning to the stories.

Likewise, organizational cultures use ritual behavior to manifest and symbolize themselves. In a school, rites might include opening day and graduation exercises, homecoming, rallies, awards assemblies, school uniforms.

School librarians should know the organization's rites and incorporate them in library activities to win school support and to forward the library's objectives. For example, a library statue might don the school T-shirt during Spirit Week, or the library could be a major drop-off point for a school's annual canned goods drive.

Special rites can operate independently in the library to give the library a powerful mystique. Here are a few suggestions:

- *Rite of passage:* orientation programs, introductory videos, training and issuance of library aide or media expert cards.
- *Rite of recognition:* library service awards, Student of the Week photo.
- *Rite of integration:* party for staff and volunteers, display of all library workers, read-aloud event.
- *Rite of style:* use of displays and plants in the library, tacit dress code, consistent look of library publications.

Site-Based Management and Restructuring

Several factors have led to the paradigm shift that has affected education: changes in family structure, change in ethnic distribution, the rise of minorities and women in the work force, the growing gap between haves and have-nots, the impact of information technology, and foreign competition.

The publication of *A Nation at Risk* in 1983 was the wake-up call for much of education. It advocated a complete overhaul of the public education system. School libraries, partly because they were overlooked in the document, rose to challenge the findings and sought to improve their own programs.

In the process of educational self-examination in light of these changes and challenges, the terms "site-based management" and "restructuring" have come into frequent use. The first affirms the strong role that building-level principals have in establishing a climate for learning. The second term refers to the task of reviewing the entire educational process and reconfiguring the system to best accomplish teaching and learning.

Restructuring can involve designing student-centered curriculum, creating "family groups" within a school, changing scheduling and length of the school day and year, regrouping teaching assignments, or developing cooperative course offerings between schools.

The core issue, though, is change. While positive change can result in added status and better environment, schools tend to resist change because it threatens the existing structure of power and influence and because it tends to redistribute limited resources. The timing may be poor, leadership may be weak, and individuals may feel personal loss. Leaders have to help the organization overcome these fears by personally building pressure for change, lowering resistance, and redirecting human forces. Both task and social aspects of change must be addressed: People must first be aware of the change, be interested in it, evaluate and try the change, and only then adopt it.

A basic change model outlines what leaders must do to bring about positive change:

- Determine the need and desire for change.
- Prepare a tentative plan with clear goals and an orderly process.
- Anticipate probable reactions to change.
- Make final decisions and set a timetable for action, but listen for input.
- Communicate the change.
- Only then, implement the change.

Even after change is adopted, follow-up activities must occur to ensure permanent acceptance and effectiveness:

- Develop supportive organizational structures: staffing, space, funding, equipment.
- Maintain awareness of the consequences of change and plan accordingly to meet individual and group needs.
- Train for knowledge and attitude: demonstrate, model, clarify, observe, give feedback, reinforce.
- Monitor: collect data, assess the change, make modifications.
- Communicate: both within the school and throughout the community.

School librarians operate on two levels: as creators of change and as those affected by change. On both levels, school librarians need to be highly involved in the change process since it ultimately affects library service. Maintaining an open, objective mindset is probably the best approach. Thorough planning, even planning to compensate for a negative change, such as budget reduction, is vital for library success.

Particularly since change affects school structure and culture, the librarian must adjust practice to accommodate it. Otherwise, the library will be left out of the organization loop and become ineffective. School librarians should adopt the role of the folktale reformer-hero rather than Rip Van Winkle, who slept through his contemporaries' era of progress.

A Matter of Style

Remember the king who disguised himself as a beggar, wandering the countryside to discover how his people really behaved? He used what he found out to choose trustworthy people to help him rule the land. Recall the princess who had to choose among different kings? She gave each man a test to measure his values and behaviors and chose the one who best matched her own personality and needs. Folklore contains many styles of leadership. Although a person automatically develops a preferred leadership style, a way to get others to work toward some goal, different situations call for specific types of leaders.

First, leadership style can be examined relative to decision-making. Is it leader-centered or group-centered. With the former approach, control and responsibility lie with the leader. In contrast, a group-centered leader shares control and responsibility with others and encourages them to express their feelings and needs.

Leadership to a great extent deals with relationships, and to some extent, the work environment dictates leadership style. The librarian leader needs to align leadership style with organizational atmosphere, or people will not relate to him and will not adopt and work for his objectives. For example, in an organization focused on management, the successful leader looks for stability and structure. Conversely, a setting based on vision and change requires a leader who favors an unstructured approach and seeks long-term results. Where vacillation characterizes an organization, the leader tends to be reactive and uncertain; a sense that stability is elusive and crisis is imminent mark that leadership style. In a balanced environment, the successful leader can plan systematic change. Organizational culture builds on a strong foundation.

Situational leadership, a recent development in leadership style theory, acknowledges the dynamic, changing nature of organizations. Different styles of leadership are called for, depending on the organization's environment and the staff's characteristics. Hersey and Blanchard's model looks at task and relationship or social dimensions within an organization. How those factors interact determines the most successful leadership style. For example:

- Where task is important and colleagiality is low, the leader should be *authoritative, a crisis manager*, telling subordinates specifically what to do.
- Where task and social atmosphere are both important, the leader needs to be *persuasive*, "selling" the vision.
- Where social and emotional support are high and task importance is low, the leader needs to concentrate on *participating* as an equal within the group and *facilitating* change.
- Finally, when the task is less specific and relationships are not critical, then the leader can *delegate* the work to self-starters. School environments exist along this entire spectrum. However, as staff grow in experience, leaders tend to change from authoritarian in the beginning to delegator, ultimately.

In the final analysis, the librarian leader must hone leadership style based on personal and organizational characteristics as well as on situational and task needs. Leadership style should be a conscious decision. Merely responding to organization culture or the flow of events is, in effect, abdicating the role of leader to others. Remember that even Cinderella realized when it was time to change her mode of operation!

Notes

Section 5

The Magic of Power and Empowerment

Power shows the man.

Aristotle

There is but one just use of power, and it is to serve people.

George Bush

Any time you think you have influence, try ordering around someone else's dog.

Sign in Cockle Bar, a London pub

As a boy, Arthur was apprenticed to Merlin, a fantastic if somewhat unconventional wizard. Under Merlin's tutelage, Arthur experienced nature's power firsthand, having been transformed into various animals to fight for survival. With the ritualistic assistance of the sword, Arthur was transformed into a powerful leader. Merlin also taught Arthur that power should be shared and that others could be transformed through that process.

Power is a magical commodity! In the hands of a competent and visionary leader, the uses of power—including the empowerment of others—can transform a school into a vital part of the community. This chapter will explore the bases for power, the means to achieve it, and ways to empower others.

Power Bases

Power is the capacity to influence others. Using an analogy from physics, power may be defined as "the ability to act or produce an effect." (Webster's *Ninth New Collegiate Dictionary*) Thus, a leader has the power to get things done. Note that power is not good or bad, it just *is*. *Rather,* how a person *uses* power becomes a value judgment.

Leadership power assumes several forms:

- *Legitimate power,* which is associated with a person's position within the organization. It can be given status through titles (director, supervisor).
- *Reward or coercive power,* which arises from the ability to reward and punish others based on their response to one's requests.
- *Expert power,* which is based on a person's skill and knowledge.
- *Referrent power,* which is based on one's personal attractiveness or appeal (charisma) or one's connection with another powerful person.

Power is derived from a person's outside resources or one's own traits. However, power becomes effective only if it is recognized and accepted by others: the targets of influence. For power to work, both the person wielding the power and the people being influenced must feel that their needs are being satisfied: a win-win situation.

Usually, the organization reinforces existing power with position and reward. However, if no one knows about the school librarian's expertise, for example, then that expertise will probably be undervalued and underused. Alternatively, if the library director holds a high position in the organizational chart and does little to earn that position, both the person and the title will lose credibility.

Power Uses

Power may be used in several ways, any of which may be at the disposal of the school librarian. Generally, power is played out either within the formal, structured system or the informal, politicized network. Both systems exist to achieve institutional goals.

- *Organizational* power enables one to make decisions where policies do not exist; the position provides the authority to influence outcomes.
- *Political* power involves influencing others and events in order to meet individual or territorial needs and goals.
- *Social* power works in relation to other people. It is relative in nature as opposed to absolute organizational power.

Power is especially significant in times of flux: where goals are unclear or unsupported, where organizational unity is lacking, or where communication is inadequate.

In order to have power, you must understand its particular manifestation in your setting. By knowing who has power, you can determine where you need to align yourself in order to carry out library goals and develop library-based leadership. The following exercise helps you analyze the power structure in your school, and enables you to plan a powerful course of action.

- Start by charting in standard hierarchical form the formal system at the school site (or district). Draw a circle to designate each person.
- On the chart indicate with dotted lines those individuals with whom your head administrator (principal, director, superintendent) most frequently interacts: superiors, peers, subordinates. What is that person's relative strength of power? What is your relationship with the head administrator?
- Next, diagram the social or informal power in your organization. Draw a line between yourself and each person in the organization, indicating the quantity of interaction by the line's thickness. Shade each person according to the degree of friendship that you have with her or him. Indicate with a small circle the degree of openness of each person (i.e., black circle implies total rigidity). You can create a more complete picture by drawing interaction lines among *all* persons.

- Compare the two systems, formal and informal. What patterns emerge? What power do you the librarian exert? What is the basis of that power? How is that power used? What can be done to empower the library?

Getting Power

Once you know your power base within the setting's power structures, you can develop your power skills. Here are some tactics that work:

- Don't feel that you have to be liked by everyone. The more powerful you are, the more likely you will make a decision that disappoints someone. You *can* be *respected* by most people, though.
- While details do matter, the final deal is what counts. Don't get so bogged down with pettiness that you forget the big picture.
- Develop a confident speaking manner: well-modulated, clear, and specific. Participate in Toastmaster's Clubs or other speakers' groups to hone your skills.
- Use space as power. Stand or take the higher position when talking with people. Have your back face the window. Face the door. Read body gesture books for clues to power moves.
- Accept help from others; it shows they're investing in you.
- Use information as power. Share tidbits that encourage others to seek your help for the rest of the story. Learn from others.
- Learn the "lingo." Does the principal use sports terms? Do computer words litter the verbal landscape? Use them to communicate your ideas with those in power.
- Track down budget facts. It helps you learn school priorities and enables you to build a stronger case the next time you ask for funds.
- Be a team player, but know when to take risks. Follow Joe Montana's example of knowing when to act in union and when to act alone.
- Make the school—and your boss—look good.
- Don't sabotage another's power. It'll come back to haunt you. Rather, play on your own strengths.

A Word About Mentors

Mentoring is like having a private coach who can teach you the game and pass on the mantle of leadership (or laser as with Luke Skywalker's mentor). Mentors provide skills and relationships that improve their protégés' abilities. Mentorship also involves changing attitudes; the protégé develops a greater sense of self-esteem and personal power. In fact, part of the mentoring relationship involves the break from the mentor as the protégé becomes a self-sufficient and mature power figure.

While natural mentoring exists within organizations, such as a district librarian helping neophyte site librarians, purposeful mentoring maximizes its benefits. Such grooming usually follows these stages: recognition of potential, trust-building, cultivation and transfer of knowledge, separation, and redefinition of relationship.

For mentorship to succeed, several features must exist:
- Organizational support,
- Volunteer participation and separation,
- Appropriate match between mentor and protégé, and
- Appropriate training and coaching. (Flaxman, p. 49-51)

Mentoring has historically been linked with the "old boy network"; yet it needs to become more inclusive to empower a diverse population of potential librarian leaders.

Just as the old king made way for the young, just as the fairy godmother helped Cinderella get the prince, so you the school librarian can promote the growth of your school community members—and empower yourself in the process.

Power of the Sexes

As a greater number of women attain supervisory positions, the issue of gender-linked power arises. In the past, women tended to copy their male counterparts' approach to power. Feminine behavior was frowned upon, and worthwhile leadership traits were suppressed. In recent times, as power has been redefined and broadened in scope, principles considered to be feminine have become accepted and valued.

An analysis of current styles indicates that women generally use a more democratic approach to decision-making. Values of inclusion and connections fit the needs of a more culturally diverse population. A caring climate and intuitive thinking style also suit the collegial style of schools. Men and women would do well to examine their gender-typical traits and incorporate both so-called male and female approaches to power.

Still, women seeking power do face specific challenges because of their societal upbringing. Recognizing that most school librarians *are* female, the following tips can help you advance and take control of your career, although these points are equally applicable to men:
- Identify where you are and where you want to go—and how to get there.
- Carefully analyze your career benefits and costs, both financial (day care, transportation) and relational (such as time with family and friends). Find ways to weave together your career and the rest of your life.
- Start out right: Learn the ropes and the people. Establish your credibility.
- Identify key people and develop good working relationships with them. Network.
- Clarify your and your staff's tasks and responsibilities.
- Learn to delegate and trust people. Help and be helped.
- Get and use information effectively.
- Deal with positive and negative feedback, both giving and receiving it.
- Take calculated risks, and accept the unknown.
- Initiate action to guarantee a non-sexist atmosphere.

- Establish a self-confident mindset of power; envision status, high regard and respect, influence, success. (Henning, p. 180-186)

"You can be both powerful and feminine, but it takes work and experimentation." (Heim, 1992, p. 130)

Power Conflicts

Where two or more people are gathered, a power relationship exists, either equal or unequal. And that power can be in conflict for a number of reasons:

- *Facts:* People have different facts or different perceptions or interpretations of the facts.
- *Goals:* Objectives differ; identification of tasks differs.
- *Methods:* People prefer different strategies or modes of behavior.
- *Values:* People's ethics and sense of justice vary.
- *Needs:* People have different needs and motives; roles differ.

The best approach to power conflicts is to establish an atmosphere that minimizes opportunities for conflict. Here are some precautions you, as a person in power, can institute:

- Encourage equal-status power relations.
- Break down stereotypes and promote intergroup relations.
- Help people build self-esteem.
- Develop superordinate goals, ones that require everyone's joint effort.
- Model even temperament in stress and conflict situations.

Power conflict in some form, though, is inevitable, so you need to deal with differences successfully. Personality clashes, particularly, call for specific steps:

- Schedule a time to confront the individual.
- Define and limit the area of conflict and the stakes at hand.
- Let each person express his or her positions and feelings. Listen actively and paraphrase to ensure understanding. Pay attention to nonverbal messages.
- Deal with the present situation and behavior, not values or attitudes.
- Find areas of overlap and possible compromise.
- Assess the meeting's effectiveness.

Some differences are not worth confronting, so choose your "battles" wisely. However, avoidance does not solve problems. The more you can deal with power issues competently in a timely manner, the less you will experience power struggles in the future.

Transactional vs Transformational Power

A classic approach to power is transactional: an even exchange of services for benefits. Analogous to Kohlberg's second level of moral development, it works on the basis of "you pat my back, I'll pat yours." Transactional power takes advantage of referent and legitimate power as it focuses on fulfilling role expectations within the system. And it supports the status quo. Relative to the library, transactional power works like this: "If you schedule your class ahead of time, you get the best choice of books."

Transformational power, in contrast, involves change rather than equilibrium. Effort is concentrated on new directions and job growth. Transformational power is associated with higher levels of Kohlberg and Maslov. It emphasizes vision rather than operational expediencies. It focuses on staff potential rather than existing job experiences. It gives a sense of purpose and encourages others to find solutions to make that purpose a reality. Transforming power implies that followers will be transformed into leaders; they are empowered. Interestingly, through transformational power, the one who *shares* power actually *gains* power.

If a transactional power structure is envisioned as a pyramid, with the boss on the top giving directions to the broad foundation of employees, then an empowering structure can be envisioned as a circle with the student at the center; people work cooperatively, the leader acting as an energizer.

Empowerment

What does empowerment look like? It assumes that employees are responsible not only for their own functions but for making the entire organization work. It supports creativity and professional growth to better satisfy the clientele. It emphasizes an organization-wide perspective rather than a job slot attitude. Everyone is learning and making decisions; the process is as important as the result.

What are signs of empowerment?
- Clarity of purpose. People know where they stand, and what their responsibilities are.
- High morale.
- A sense of fairness and trust.
- Recognition for effort and results.
- A sense of teamwork where the whole is greater than the parts.
- High participation in input, decision-making, and implementation.
- An atmosphere of learning.
- Clear, timely, and adequate communication. (Scott, p. 24-25)

What are optimum conditions for empowerment?
- Helpful structures and systems.
- Personal character: integrity, maturity, an abundance of ideas.
- Skills: communication, planning, problem-solving.
- Self-direction, -motivation, -monitoring.
- Adequate resources: human, budgetary, structural. (Covey, p. 197)

What does an empowering leader do?
- Offers a vision that is inspiring, meaningful, and "owned" by everyone.
- Enables others rather than controls them.
- Shares information and links groups.
- Understands the difficulties of change, and facilitates others' acceptance of growth experiences.

How can librarians empower others?
- Communicate a vision of the library and offer ways to make that vision a reality.

- Promote student and staff growth through skills development.
- Encourage broad-based decision-making.

The benefits of empowerment are many. With self-direction come fewer discipline problems. With empowerment comes a feeling of success — and a positive atmosphere. With ownership comes a great sense of responsibility and service. With empowerment the library can forge ahead with greater, broad-based power.

<u>Notes</u>

Section 6

Leading the Library: The Inner Ring of Leadership

When the best leader's work is done, the people say: 'We did it ourselves!"

Lao-tzu

When librarians meet at conferences, they always have stories to tell. There's the library assistant who paints a school bus mural in the library to liven the place. There's the ostracized student who experiences her first academic success by using the library's computers. There's the student who researches day and night ways to network the library. There's the teacher who publicly raves about the librarian and consistently plans units with her. There's the board member who pushes for an additional permanent staff position. There's the bus driver who donates two-year subscriptions to library periodicals so students will read on the ride. There's the principal who fights for a new library building. All true stories told by school librarians.

What story do *you* have to tell about your library? Could you enthrall an audience with the excitement and suspense, the humor and the inspiration of your library? The best storytelling involves a good story and a good delivery. This section helps you create that story through strong leadership. You can attain the first ring of power: in the library.

Okay, take out your library calendar, your time manager, your datebook. What does it look like? Is it filled with class visits? Are periods blocked out for teacher planning and evaluation conferences? What library programs dot the months? Are parent group events included? What committee charges are reflected on it: departmental, schoolwide, districtwide, regional, professional? What in-services and workshops are indicated for you and your staff? Are times allotted for public relations, budgeting, and collection development? What is happening in your library? And is the library the heart and intellectual center of the school?

The Vision Thing

"To go where no one has traveled, to lead where no one has gone." While images of Star Trek may dance in your head at the thought of vision, a well-designed and encompassing long-range idea of what you want to see happen in the library is a must for strong leadership in the library.

Recently one of my 14-going-on-41 students was discussing technology for the library. "Dr. Farmer, where do you want the library to be in five years? Just tell me your vision, and I can find and configure the equipment and connectors to make it work." And he can! I know librarians who have been given $25,000 or more outright with the condition that they spend it in a week, sometimes just on books. If a fairy godperson were to visit you tomorrow, could you articulate your vision?

For your vision of the library to become a reality, it must possess several characteristics:

- It must be *coherent*. The planning pieces must fit together logically and clearly.
- It must be *powerful* enough to command a following.
- It must be *achievable* within the realities of the umbrella organization.
- It must reflect the library's *ideal*: what it should be.
- It should include *criteria for measuring success*, such as a percentage of teachers planning and implementing information skills units in partnership with the librarian.
- It should encompass *staff roles and structures*. People are the library's principal resource and the means to make the vision a reality. (Wilson, p. 18-20)

As you analyze your vision of the library, follow these easy steps:

- Identify opportunities and obstacles by gathering and interpreting data about resources and the library's environment.
- Clarify the library's and institution's cultures and values.
- Consider alternative scenarios and solutions to problems by brainstorming with key players.
- Develop a workable vision by involving all in the input, but deciding yourself.
- Ground the vision in strategic, specific plans.
- Carry out your vision by motivating and supporting those involved.
- Evaluate results and modify plans accordingly.

Resourceful Leadership

Let's face it. The library can't be any stronger than its resources, material and human. You can have the best instructional skills and the loveliest site on campus, but if the library doesn't have adequate print and nonprint materials on hand, the library will never play a leading role in the school and education. True, with the advent of online databases, the library can expand resources beyond its four walls. But ultimately, students need to get the information in their hot little hands for it to become real.

Particularly with the increased emphasis on resource-based education, transcending the textbook, the library should have a heyday in collection development. After all, as a librarian you know that one title can help students in three or four different disciplines. A CD-ROM product such as the *Time Almanac* serves as a motivator and source of information for students 10 years old and up across the curriculum. It is that cost-effective, broad perspective that needs to be heard when resource-based learning and accompanying acquisitions budgets are discussed.

Too often, though, collection development is not done systematically. In some cases, the librarian just buys what the teacher wants. In other cases, funds are allocated for computer hardware and utility programs rather than information-rich software. Usually the missing ingredient is a strong vision of the collection, supported by thorough knowledge of currently available sources. Teachers need to see how you select materials, and they need to see how their input fits into the total library financial and collection picture. One approach is to present a few acquisition scenarios, noting the materials and costs, with the bottom line being the number of students and courses affected by each. The ultimate goal is to provide the resources necessary for all users and staff to accomplish what they need to do.

Information technology plays a prominent role in librarian leadership. Ever since the announcement of the information superhighway by Vice President Al Gore, adults and students are eager to cruise the electronic roads. The hype surrounding new technology may not give due value to the librarian's role. Some librarians may feel threatened by this new technology. But as information providers it is absolutely necessary to take a leading role in order to maintain professional credibility. Both in terms of acquiring and using these resources, librarians need to keep current with the trends. What are you doing to position the library in the forefront? Are you:

- Using the current hardware and software?
- Using telecommunications?
- Examining current trends such as networking?
- Keeping current with reviews about hardware and software?
- Acquiring general reference and cross-curricular programs?
- Teaching students and adults how to use technology effectively?
- Consistently increasing your knowledge about educational technology?
- Participating in technology planning committees at different levels, both in school and library circles?

If you are not central to the educational technology process, your library will be left behind, and students will not have the most effective access to today's and tomorrow's information.

Supervising Successfully

The other significant resource needed to implement the library vision is people. Even if you have no paid staff working with you in the library, you still should have some kind of volunteer help from students or adults for some kind of leadership to emerge. After all, a leader needs followers. How you work together will determine how the library itself "works" to serve its community.

What needs to be done? The first key to successful supervision is to *match the task with the person.* Of course, this entails an honest and open relationship with each individual so the two of you can develop a workable plan. What motivates your potential help? What needs is he hoping to meet? Those people issues need to be ironed out before tasks and structures can be addressed. Then, by listing those jobs that have to be done to achieve the vision, you can determine each person's role within the goal's context.

Next, you need to *educate* the person, not only in terms of job skills but also in terms of the library and the larger institution. What are the expectations? What are the policies? What are the underriding values of the culture? Naturally, you need to model the desired behavior.

As you train each person, certain steps will optimize results:

- Give clear directions, and provide referral manuals and visuals.
- Match training strategy with learning style. Some folks want to watch first, while others need to get their hands on the project immediately. Some people need detailed step-by-step instruction, while others just need to see the goal and can figure out the steps for themselves. Accommodate physical challenges such as eyesight, coordination, hearing.
- Begin with close supervision, having the person show you each step of the process for you to verify. Then check results each time until the person can do a good job consistently and independently. Spot-check results thereafter for long-term success.
- Be sure that the person has the resources and support to do the job well.
- When the job becomes routine, talk with the worker about possible improvements or enhancements of the task. In that way, the person can keep growing on the job.

Third, you need to *support growth* of the person. What continuing education opportunities are available to help your staff to improve their productivity and competence? Facilitate ways to enlarge their responsibilities and authority. Perhaps your subordinate has outside priorities that need to be addressed; if you help her satisfy those needs without compromising the library's and organization's needs, then the person is more likely to feel good about the job and do it better.

Fourth, you need to *correct* unproductive behavior. Disciplining can be a disagreeable task, but it results in improved staff and library outcomes. Some pointers will ease the process:

- Identify the problem: Is it yours or the other person's? Maybe you're a neatnic about desktops, and piled papers "bug" you even if the job gets done. The problem is yours. However, if your staff loses important records regularly, then the problem is the staff's.
- Document the problem factually and objectively. Determine under what conditions the problem occurs: under time restrictions? When there are crowds of people? Just before vacations? Ascertain how regularly the problem occurs.
- Examine the real problem. Is a person late because the car pool is undependable, or is lateness a result of too much partying the night before?
- Determine whether the problem is one under your control. A salary schedule might not be controllable, but hours might be negotiable.
- Speak to the person privately, confronting him or her with the facts. Try to solve the problem jointly to each other's

satisfaction. Sometimes the issue is simply one of miscommunication.

- Follow through. Review the problem with the staff to check for progress. Carry out consequences for noncompliance if necessary. Whatever you set as a standard must be enforced; otherwise, your credibility decreases — as does library productivity.

Creating a Climate for Learning

Keeping your vision of the library in mind, ask yourself, What function does the student play? What kind of groupings can be accommodated in the library? What kind of activity is encouraged? What informational resources, as well as space allocation and furniture, support the objectives of the learning environment? Think of the physical library as the stage and props for the actions of the users.

An interesting exercise is to assess with a questionnaire what faculty and students consider the ideal library environment. When their expectations match the reality of the library, user needs are most fully satisfied. Representative questions are listed here, followed by the need addressed in each query. Users rank each dimension's importance on a scale from 1 to 6. By seeing the overall patterns that emerge, you can create an atmosphere that satisfies personal and organizational needs.

In the ideal school library

1. I could get a feeling of accomplishment.   (achievement)
2. I could feel actively involved.   (activity)
3. I would receive fair treatment.   (rules)
4. I could try out my own ideas.   (creativity)
5. I could work independently of others.   (independence)
6. I could make use of my abilities.   (variety, esteem)
7. I could influence others.   (authority)
8. I could make friends with other students.   (socialization)
9. I could find what I needed if I tried.   (compensation)
10. I could use my own judgment.   (responsibility)
11. I could feel that the library was relevant.   (relevancy)
12. I could help other students.   (helping)
13. I could be "somebody" in the library.   (esteem, status)
14. I could get individual help from the staff.   (individual teaching)
15. I could do a variety of things.   (variety)
16. I could have good physical learning conditions.   (environment)

As you compare student, faculty, and library staff perceptions you can determine which expectations are congruent and determine what measures to take. For example, if students value interaction greatly and the staff doesn't, then you may need to train staff to be more responsive (particularly if you value interaction) and provide separate areas for group work so other students can work independently.

Just as in a self-contained classroom, students need to be supervised in the library so a climate of learning can exist. Here are some humane approaches to library discipline.

- Arrange the library for maximum visibility and ease of activity. Provide study areas. Offer leisure reading corners. Place the reference desk in a highly accessible area.
- Get to know students on a one-to-one and group basis. Take individual differences into account when working with students. Promote mutual respect and trust.
- Anticipate disciplinary problems and brainstorm ways to deal with them. Typical solutions include special displays that cue into pre-vacation anticipation and supplementary supervision during rainy days (especially for campus-type layouts).
- Set expectations and limits through well-defined, enforceable and fair rules. Involve students in setting these standards of behavior and defining consequences for noncompliance. Be sure that rules are consistent with the rest of the school's. Post and discuss these rules from the start. Reinforce positive behavior and provide timely corrective feedback when behavior is not appropriate.
- Use signals to discourage possible disruptive behavior: the "look," physical proximity, friendly questions.
- Provide activity. Help students get back on target by helping them locate or evaluate resources. Engage them in volunteer projects for the library. Offer a new magazine to read.
- Remove the problem. Separate students. Reassign them another seat. Provide a cooling-off period elsewhere. Confer with them separately from their peers.

Creative Curriculum Development

Since the library works in context of its setting, curriculum development and implementation comprise a major library service. Where the librarian becomes a leader is in the unfolding of that course approach to learning.

In the day-to-day implementation of the curriculum, you, the librarian, need to provide the resources and successful learning experiences in connection with that curriculum. For this to happen there are two prerequisites: You need to have the information from the teacher to acquire the needed resources, and you need to plan with teachers the best ways to deliver the course content.

You as librarian need to assert yourself as resource specialist and instructional consultant. As you plan with the teacher, you should focus on your strengths: knowledge of the information and how to evaluate it. As you sit down with teachers, follow this plan:

- Assess student outcomes: what should they learn? Consider both content and information skills.
- Determine student background : what they already know.
- Assess the resources available to give students the information they need to acquire the needed competencies.

- Establish the delivery system: where, when, time frame, instructional mode, evaluation methods.
- Implement the plan.
- Assess the results and modify the plan for future improvement.

Partnership in planning units is a first start in curriculum-related library leadership. However, the real leadership occurs at the course development stage. When you hear about a new course being offered, discuss the syllabus with the teacher and offer to order relevant resources in time for the class's first session. Particularly with the explosion in media products, you can serve a vital function as a professional evaluator and selector in the field.

Do you see a curricular need not being met? Perhaps it's multicultural studies or multimedia production. Talk with a likely teacher, brainstorming content and resource ideas. When the school curriculum takes advantage of the existing library collection, and the collection grows with the needs of the students, then the library truly works as an integral part of education.

The library has an even stronger educational base than any curriculum. Because authentic learning does not take place in discrete little compartments, the library has the advantage of being a cross-curricular center for learning. How often have you seen a student start a class assignment in the library only to spot a great resource for another course? How often have you seen a student get so involved in learning how to use a CD-ROM-based periodicals index that he doesn't get to the magazine itself—but has taught three other students how to use the technology? How often have you seen a student become drawn into a library display, and check out a book—and a booklist—on the subject? How often have you seen the one-track student doggedly look up everything on horses and along the way learn a variety of searching techniques using a wide spectrum of reference tools? Cases like these demonstrate opportunities for lifelong educational leadership within the library.

Controversy still exists about the place of information skills: Should it be taught as a separate course or integrated throughout the curriculum? It parallels the issue of computer literacy courses. Those who support the separate library skills course assert that students will then be guaranteed systematic exposure to those important skills. However, if the school truly values information literacy (and it is a "hot" term), then it behooves the administration and faculty to build learning experiences about information processing that are embedded in curriculum contexts. And it is the librarian's duty to clarify and help design an articulated program throughout the grade levels in cooperation with the curriculum development team. Particularly since information literacy is such an important skill, instruction and support resources in that area demonstrate the leadership that the librarian has within the school. Use that educational fact to your advantage. Tell the library story at every occasion.

In fact, all library activity should further information literacy: written and visual aids to teach students how to use equipment, read-aloud programs to foster leisure reading, video production workshops to train students on organization and presentation skills, booklists on bookmarks and posters to link interests and resources, "trivia" contests to hone searching strategies, hypermedia programs to teach bibliographic skills, film discussion groups to advance critical thinking, magazine cut-up areas to help students learn visually and kinesthetically, displays of student work to recognize information literacy mastery. The library should offer something for everyone, some way to inspire both students and adults to learn.

This complex application of resources is the backbone of librarian leadership and the basis on which to create a rich mythology of the library. Let your work be a heroic saga!

Section 7

Leadership Within the School: The Second Ring of Power

Leadership for school library media specialists may not mean "being out in front," but "leading from the middle."

American Library Association

Librarian Ken keeps a closet full of magic hats in his library, which he whips out depending on the occasion. He dons a mortarboard when he orients new staff or educates the faculty and administration about educational technology and other new information tools. He sports a baseball cap when he coaches students before a library presentation to the school board. He wears a top hat when he holds orientation sessions for incoming volunteer coordinators or hosts the library committee. He dons a laurel wreath when he counsels struggling staff and frustrated researchers. Ken has tossed his hat into the school political ring and juggles multiple roles as a school leader. Ken is a happy and productive librarian.

Think of the individual characters in folktales who transformed a whole town or society: the Pied Piper of Hamlin, the brave little tailor, the tailor who "sewed" the emperor's new clothes. Even though they each had little official authority, they made good use of their skills and wit to shake up the status quo.

Librarians have a special opportunity to lead the vanguard in establishing the school as a learning community. Particularly with the trend of school restructuring, the idea of school wide lifelong learning plays into the library's function and calls for the leadership of the librarian. This chapter offers ways to make the library central to the school and guides you the library leader, as you empower faculty and administrators through information. It's your chance to not only storytell the legends of success but to create them yourself. You can command the second ring of power: school leadership.

Transforming School

Whether it's in response to accreditation review or parental pressure, national outrage or student pleas, schools are examining themselves to develop the best programs possible so student outcomes will be optimized. And we school librarians need to play a central role in that process.

What are some of the solutions being offered?

- The "hot ticket item" is *restructuring.* Faculty and administrators are redesigning the curriculum and the support structure to engage students in meaningful learning experiences. Some of the issues involved in restructuring include "authentic" assessment, collaborative and other grouped teaching strategies, integrated courses, broad-based decision-making, and local control.

- *Resource-based learning* uses a variety of materials as learning stimuli for students. A librarian's dream, this approach recognizes that students have different reading levels and different learning styles and so need resources to match their interests and abilities.
- *Global/multicultural education* recognizes the contributions of peoples worldwide and the richness of diversity. It prepares students for global interdependence.
- *Integrated education* understands that learning crosses traditional disciplines and that students need to be involved both intellectually and emotionally.
- *Academic coaching* supports the idea that students need individual interventions at critical learning points. Students in effect teach themselves as they learn how to learn.
- *Portfolio assessment* uses a variety of evidence to demonstrate student learning: writing samples, benchmark projects, videotapes, tests, computer presentations.

The Librarian as CIO

One of the trendy job titles in business is chief information officer. This person organizes the company's documentation and controls its access, often using computer technology to structure information. Sounds like a librarian, yes? Except that the CIO often has more money and power than most librarians.

The school librarian is an information manager and can be the information leader in the school. As school CIOs, we need to analyze our community, their information needs and suppliers, and be their advocates using long-term planning.

Leading from the Middle

The position of school librarian is an ambiguous one relative to organizational charts. We are both teachers and administrators, both line and staff. In California, school librarianship requires both a teacher's credential and a library media specialist credential; at the district level an administrative credential is also required. With whom do we align in order to lead within the school?

Probably the best tack is to take advantage of the ambiguity and lead from the middle. Since we work with a wide variety of teachers, we can offer an objective perspective on instructional strategies and can bring different teachers together to maximize curricula. Since we work with all types of school personnel, we can serve as reality checks for decision-makers. Because our schedules are less set than other teachers we can work on committees and special projects that need flexible meeting time. And because we connect with others beyond the building level, we can foster broad-based education.

A key factor in leading from the middle is communication. We are, after all, information processors, so communication is for us a natural way of working. Communicating from the middle necessitates both active listening and effective sharing of information. The more input we get from different constituents, the more effectively we can interpret and synthesize the information and pass it on.

Working with Administration

Usually the school librarian is directly accountable to the principal and dean of faculty. Particularly when dealing with cross-curricular issues, the school librarian needs to communicate effectively with the principal. The major obstacle to a good working relationship is usually a lack of knowledge about each other's expectations.

With the advent of site-based management, the pivotal role of the principal has been acknowledged. The principal really does set the tone of the school. What the principal considers important is what happens. No matter how strong a union or academic council is, the principal can circumvent the organization to accomplish personal priorities (though he or she may have to "pay" for it afterwards). Particularly at the elementary level, if the principal wants to see technology, then the library will have computers. If the principal hates audiovisuals probably the library will concentrate on print matter. If the principal is authoritarian and believes in compartmentalization, then less team-teaching and team–planning will occur.

It is of paramount importance for you, the school librarian, to know what is important to the principal and how she operates with people. As much as possible, you need to match the principal's style, be it one-to-one conversations or monthly written reports. You need to make sure the principal's agenda is carried out in the library before you take on additional, possibly risk-taking projects for the library. Using your librarian expertise, do something that addresses the principal's priorities: research year-round school schedules, design network structures, send monthly reports, find high-potential grants. Then improve the library concretely in a way that supports the principal's vision. In other words, model the kind of partnership that you want with the principal.

Often the principal does not have a clear picture of the library and its potential. If he is open to change, then you have a golden chance to educate the principal and get him on your side. For the library to be a leading component in the school, the principal needs to possess certain library-related competencies:

- Information literacy,
- Cooperative model of planning and implementation,
- Establishment and maintenance of a learning environment,
- Familiarity with a wide variety of media, including computer technology, as tools and resources.

Show what is possible in the library through school librarian documents about model programs. Keep the principal informed about ALA's *Information Power* and its spin-offs. Send copies of your team-teacher lesson plans and student outcomes. Give a presentation of technology's benefits in student learning. These site-based experiences open the way for your administrators to learn about the library and support its growth.

Peer Relations

School librarians should be considered to be on a par with other teachers. If they are not, then before you can even consider peer leadership, you must show that you are an equal partner in the educational process. Some teachers don't realize the educational background of librarians; a few well-placed degrees and framed credentials can act as subtle signals of your professionalism.

More important, though, is your action within the library and in other situations with teachers. Do you:

- Teach groups of students in front of teachers?
- Let teachers know about recent library acquisitions?
- Produce book lists and research guides in their course of study?
- Conduct inservice training for teachers?
- Research educational issues that affect teaching?
- Acquire professional teacher resources?
- Help teachers and students produce audiovisual aids?

Once your professional credibility is established, then you can proceed to work collaboratively with teachers as peers. Collaboration transcends the library; it encompasses the development and achievement of schoolwide goals and objectives. Whether planning an assembly or participating in an accreditation school self-study, your professional approach to education can help you grow as a peer leader.

Here are some tips to successful collaboration:

- Know the direction you want to go. If you are unclear about the issues involved, dig up the facts from knowledgeable associates.
- Build relationships and alliances. Discover the key players and their priorities, and find out how you can help them.
- Disarm the opposition. Understand where potential opponents stand—and why. Get their perspectives and learn from them.
- Work towards "win-win" situations when problem-solving. Keep in mind the ultimate objective: student outcomes.

An interesting exercise as you try to advance the library agenda within the context of school workings is to identify people's roles through the CAIRO process. Say you want to network library resources with the intent that those sources can be made available to everyone throughout the school.

- Identify who has to be *Consulted*.
- Identify who has the right to *Approve* or disapprove.
- Identify who needs to be kept *Informed*.
- Identify who is ultimately *Responsible* for the outcome, for getting it done.
- Identify who is *Out* of the information loop. (Bolman, p. 32, 59)

This process is useful for all types of collaboration, for it reveals the human and organizational dimensions of decision-making.

A third step in peer relations is peer appraisal. As we school librarians observe teachers in the library, we can compare teaching strategies and tell which are effective. In addition, as we instruct and supervise others, we hone our own teaching strategies. Few other teachers are in that position, so school librarians can take advantage of that opportunity and act as mentors, coaching others.

In that coaching role, school librarians give special encouragement on an individual basis. In order to improve teacher performance and increase self-confidence, school librarians explain needed skills with enthusiasm and encouragement. In the process, school librarians listen to teachers' needs and suggest corrections as appropriate.

As peer appraisers, school librarians perform specific tasks:
- Ask probing questions about teacher practice,
- Maintain a supportive atmosphere, and
- Keep goals manageable.

Working with Parents and Other Adults

One goal within the school structure is to encourage involved, supportive parents who contribute time, talents, and ideas to assist the school in reaching its goals. By furthering that goal, you help build the kind of support that will pay off in the library as well. The underlying philosophy as you deal with parents should be "We both want the best for your child."

Parents choose to contribute to schools for several reasons:
- Personal reward;
- A sense of belonging, a social experience;
- A sense that they make a difference, that they are useful;
- An interest in their own and other children;
- A sense of responsibility: the moral good, citizenship;
- A sense of self-improvement; and
- A need for recreation and fun!

Very practical factors can make the difference between support and apathy. Here are some ways you can help:
- *Transportation:* Can you pick up a parent on the way to or from work?
- *Child care:* Can a student library aide supervise their children? Could you set up a story hour?
- *Communication:* Can you participate in a telephone tree? Can you help produce a parent newsletter, or translate it for non-English readers?
- *Work conditions*: Do you have a corner where parents can take a break? Is the library available to parent work groups part of the day or during off-hours?

Of course, parents respond even more positively if *you* support *them*. By attending parent association meetings, participating in activities with them, and assisting them whenever feasible, you build a valuable support base while legitimately recognizing their importance.

Information Literacy: The Librarian's Shingle

What is your niche? What special talents do you have within the school community? The cornerstone of the school library program—and school librarian leadership—is information literacy. The information literate person is able to access, evaluate, and use information. As you model its educational potential, you can use information literacy as a power base for working with teachers and administrators.

Several national reports on education reinforce the importance of information literacy:

- The National Commission on Excellence in Education, in their 1983 report *A Nation at Risk*, urged an alliance of home, school, and library in order to attain excellence in education and a learning society. (U. S. Dept. of Education, p. iii)
- The SCANS Report, by the U. S. Department of Labor, outlines the skills that students need to compete successfully in the business world. Linked with information literacy, they include foundation skills of reading, thinking, and self-management as well as competencies in resource allocation, information processing, use of technology, collaboration, and systems analysis. (Packer, p. 28)
- The 1986 Carnegie Foundation Report noted that "The quality of a college is measured by the resources for learning on the campus and the extent to which students become independent, self-directed learners." (ALA, Information Literacy, p. 6)

School librarians might well say, "There they go; I must go after them, for I am their leader!" While the Information Age has been touted now for some years, school librarians are still occasionally left behind in the educational dust. We certainly corner the market on access and use of information. We need to take advantage of this professional door of opportunity.

What are some ways that you can make information literacy an integral part of the school?

- Be a central player in school restructuring, particularly as it applies to the learning process.
- Provide leadership in curriculum development and educational technology related to information literacy.
- Promote resource-based learning.
- Acquire interactive educational software and other technological resources that engage student learning.
- Disseminate research on the impact of information skills on student performance.
- Conduct inservice workshops for teachers on information literacy.

Librarian Contributions

Using your professional skills, you can contribute significantly to school improvement in several ways:

- You can develop a local *database* of needed sources of help: for jobs and volunteer positions, personal needs, educational and recreational opportunities.
- You can *introduce educational technology* by showing model school projects in other settings, establishing a review center, troubleshooting technical programs, and incorporating your library collection into the curriculum.
- You can *advise a group of students*, either for academic counseling or to support an interest group such as Video Club or the school newspaper. Not only do you become more involved in the school and provide a needed service, but students see you in a different light; you are not just the person with the answers or the book-stamper.
- You can *conduct content-based workshops* for teachers. For

example, you can model resource-based learning by showing how to locate and evaluate information on social justice issues that can then be the basis for positive social action.

- You can help the school find valuable *funding sources* by researching grant sources. In some cases the librarian has written or helped write grant proposals for the school, especially if a library component plays a significant part. You can even auction off your researching skills as part of a school fund-raising event.
- You can *research issues* that your school is grappling with, such as year-round scheduling or single-sex instruction. You can do a background literature search, making use of online databases as well as maintaining a clipping file of current topics under discussion.
- You can provide background information and a space for *public debate* about current issues, thereby dramatically demonstrating that the library is an open center for information.
- You can vanguard *intellectual freedom* campaigns to safeguard teachers' freedom to instruct and students' freedom to learn, as well as the library's freedom to provide ideas from all walks of life.
- You can help students and teachers *produce audiovisual aids*, such as videotapes and transparencies or dry mounts. To do this requires warehousing the relevant equipment and knowing how to use it. Unless audiovisual productions are a part of your job description, it is probably better to show others how to create their own work; in that way, you are teaching them another informational skill.
- You can *display* student work and library resources related to school activities, such as Black History Month or Safe and Sober Graduation.
- You can have library aides *videotape* school events, keeping a permanent copy in the library.
- You can establish and maintain school *archives* of student publications, playbills, and other historically important artifacts. One library creates and displays posters about significant school alumnae, which always attracts attention.
- You can connect the school with the world by *linking with other information sources.*
- You can act as a *liaison* between the public library and the school, communicating class resource needs.

Naturally, you can use other skills to help the school. Perhaps you are a good editor or a good baker. Both contributions are welcome. Helping with school bond campaigns, chaperoning dances, sponsoring student productions— all are ways that show you care about the school and mark you as a potential leader.

Committees

Your participation and leadership in school committees make you a significant part of the school community and a decided asset to the library. Committees constitute the backbone of school information-gathering and recommending, if not outright decision-making. It seems obvious that we school librarians should play a leading role in committees because of our knowledge of students, teachers, administrators, and curriculum and because of our ability to gather and interpret data.

If you have never worked on a committee, then here are some tips to make your first experience a successful one that will lead to other task assignments:

- If possible, choose a committee that you care about. Perhaps it's curricular-based and focused on staff development. Maybe you really like sports; then an athletics committee might be the ticket for you. It shows you in a different light and demonstrates that you're not a single-issue person. The point is, you will be working with others for an extended period of time, so you'll want to enjoy digging into the subject.

- If possible, choose a committee that makes a difference, one that doesn't merely rubber stamp someone's opinion. In that way you can use your research skills to advantage. (Also, it does feel good to know that your work will be rewarded.)

- Do your homework. Dig up the background; find out what's the core issue; gather relevant information. Do whatever committee assignments are given you, even if they seem trivial, like collating papers and making lists. Make sure you come prepared for each meeting with all the documentation you need.

- Follow meeting protocol. Arrive on time or a bit early. Offer to help set up. Know appropriate parliamentary procedures. Participate and listen attentively. Keep on task. Keep notes. Get to know the other members, and how they work. (Remember the power structure?) Be fair, courteous, and objective. Come without hidden agendas. Stay the whole meeting, and help clean up afterwards.

- When speaking, talk clearly and accurately. Make sure everyone can hear you, and that your voice is pleasant to hear. Make your point, and justify it efficiently. Use visual aids if appropriate.

- If you lead a meeting, remember that your first task is to facilitate decision-making. Prepare an agenda with group-initiated items and time frame, and distribute it ahead of time so members can prepare. Include background papers as appropriate.

- Be sure the meeting room arrangements are made, including equipment and provision of beverage and optional food.

- Begin and end on time. Ensure that a pro-active, responsive, and respectful working atmosphere prevails.

- Respect confidentialities.

- Have someone record significant points for all to see; it provides a concrete measure of group progress.

- Monitor the group: keep them on task and stimulated.

- Make sure everyone has opportunities to speak, and summarize group findings.

- Make sure everyone has a task and knows its parameters.

- Thank everyone for participating, and follow up on any necessary details.

When speaking on behalf of a committee, remember that you are its representative, so you should abide by the group's decisions and support them. However, as their leader, you can wield power to influence the group during the meeting so that their decisions will coincide with your own stance.

Communicating

Within the library, most communication is impromptu or procedural, such as immediate directions or permanent manuals. However, with relation to the rest of the school, communication becomes much more complex. Especially as more people consider your information, you need to make it professional in content and appearance.

Library communication within the school and to the outside community should have a unified look that reflects the library's image. Create a library logo, which might be adopted from national library clip art or customized to fit your library's setting. Perhaps students can create a logo as a library contest. A consistent "look" of graphics, layout, and paper provides a distinct visual memory of the library that will enhance your message.

For a particular communique, you obviously want to *convey your message clearly and succinctly* so the recipient can understand and take action on it. If you are in doubt about what you want to convey, talk it over with a colleague first to help crystallize your ideas. If you have problems with language niceties, use your English experts as consultants. Also consider sending your message in other languages as appropriate to your community. That you make the effort to be inclusive and respectful of other cultures demonstrates that you care.

Next, you need to *consider the target audience:* students, teachers, administration, staff, parents, community. Will your message have wide circulation, or will it be addressed to a select few? The more you know about the audience, the more you can customize your message to match their interests. For example, you can do a fun "hip hop" message to students about a library event, which wouldn't work as well with parents. For a Friends of the Library reception you might produce a high-quality formal invitation. For a general message to the entire school community, you probably want to sound professional and positive.

Another important step is to *choose the appropriate format:* written, oral, visual, multimedia. Each has its place and function. The following list of possible formats will help you determine which will convey your message most effectively:

- *Memos* provide quick reminders.
- *Reports* state the library's cause in depth.
- *Brochures* build awareness about the library and complement presentations.
- *Posters* serve as quick reminders and as one-stop learning stations.
- *Newsletters* inform interest groups of progress and upcoming events and can be used to announce library needs.
- *Press releases* send the library's message to the "world."
- *Displays* constitute the basic multimedia communication tool since they combine visuals and text and can incorporate movement or simulations.

- *Slide-tape shows* are portable and can be changed or modified fairly easily to fit a specific audience. They literally transport a setting to another location.
- *Videotapes* dramatize and simulate library and school needs—and successes.
- *Speeches* make a personal statement about issues and enable the audience to respond immediately. (Farmer, 1993, p. 88)

Whatever the communication, it should be professional in content and appearance. Like clothing, communication conveys an instant image. It should be well-timed: in advance so that people can act upon it, close enough to the time of action so people don't forget about it. If your communication is crucial, deliver it in person. That individual touch still makes a significant difference. And, of course, keep communicating on a regular basis so people will see you and the library as an ongoing, integral part of the school.

All the School's a Stage

In the final analysis, being a leader in the school is a testimony to others' belief in you and a decided responsibility to empower others because you believe in them. While you can study organizational and personal chains of influence to optimize your leadership potential, while you can analyze your power bases and mold your leadership style, the real base for systemic leadership is a credible, professional working relationship with the school community. As you support the school, you develop a stronger, more broad-based support system to help you lead.

As a final mental check, give yourself an audition. Ask yourself:
- What roles are you trying out for?
- What roles have you played successfully?
- How have you prepared for the role?
- What makes you stand out from the rest?
- How well do you present yourself?
- Are you willing to show up at all rehearsals (planning meetings)?
- How well do you get along with the rest of the cast?
- Can you work well under the director (principal)?
- Will you give your all?
- Are you ready for center stage?

Section 8

Leadership Within the Community: The Third Ring of Power

One hand washes the other; give and take.

Epicharmus

Do not separate yourself from the community.

Hillel

I love being a school librarian in the community in which I live. My commute is wonderfully short—just two miles—and living close to school makes it easy to attend after-school student events. I get to see "my" students and volunteers in the local shopping malls, parks, and church (they are occasionally surprised to see that the librarian has another life). I have a steady source of baby sitters, not to be undervalued these days. My son will experience his mom as his high school librarian, and in the meantime I know his present librarian on both a professional and personal basis. Girl Scout leaders whom I trained have children attending my school—another connection.

The same library I use during busman's holidays is the one I call about upcoming assignments. I can browse my local bookstores after school knowing that they'll give a good discount. And I can count on my neighbors to help, both as regular volunteers and as crisis-time campaigners for library issues. The result is a holistic approach to librarianship, which I greatly value.

As school librarians we operate within the broader community as well as within the library. Some of us hold allegiance to two communities: the one in which we work and the one in which we reside. Some of us commute; others are privileged to work and play in the same area. In either case, we can be seen as professionals at any time (rather like the doctor who gets asked for free medical diagnoses during cocktail parties).

Have you ever been asked, "Oh, since you're a librarian, could you organize the church library?" or "Since you're a school librarian, I bet you'd teach my Girl Scout troop how to do storytelling!" While there may be times that you want to say, "Enough, already! I just do library work when I get paid—between 8 and 4," you can take that public image and make it work for you and your library.

And, indeed, you have the responsibility to support and improve your community. As Thomas Jefferson wrote, "A democratic society depends upon an informed and educated citizenry." Those information and education skills give you potential power to help shape the community the way you see best benefits everyone. ALA Past President Patricia Glass Schuman has pointed out that "libraries are the only institutions in our society whose underlying social *purpose* is to collect, organize, and provide access to information." (ALA, 1985, p. 15)

This chapter reveals the challenges of the community and shows you how to attain the third ring of power in that setting.

Building Relationships

Now is the time to self-check your relations with local libraries. As you do this self-inventory, mark those items that merit more time and effort. Remember, by strengthening your professional contacts you are providing better service to your school through resource-sharing, cross-instruction, and professional development.

How Do You Relate to Local Libraries?
- Do you have a list of local school, public, government, and special libraries? Do you know their librarians?
- Do you communicate regularly with local school and public librarians?
- Do you let public libraries know about major research assignments?
- Do you exchange library holdings lists of periodicals, indexes, special collections, or nonprint items? Do you create union lists of these resources?
- Do you exchange booklists or instructional aids, either librarian- or teacher-generated?
- Do you help each other with collection development through reviewing, exchanging, donations, group purchasing, or collection specialization?
- Do you publicize each other's activities?
- Do you do joint programming: sharing speakers, displays, equipment?
- Do you tell students about opportunities at other libraries, either for work or recreation?
- Do you share professional materials or conference insights?
- Do you train one another or facilitate group professional development?
- Do you support one another in library issues, such as school campaigns or library bonds?

As you can see, the opportunities for improved library service *throughout* the community can increase dramatically when librarians form strong working relationships among themselves. And this model of collaboration transfers to your relationship with other community groups.

Do you have a directory of community institutions and organizations: business service groups, local governmental agencies, educational sources, volunteer groups, nonprofit organizations, youth programs, and recreational centers? How many of these groups serve youth directly or indirectly? These are potential community partners, which you can cultivate. Besides offering valuable resources, community groups are credible channels of communication, often to targeted student populations.

Here are some ways that you can create positive relationships and foster mutual support:

- *Build on* existing structures. If your school has an established tie with local business, talk with your administrators to see how you can fit into the picture, acting as a school ambassador or liaison to them.
- *Develop* a local youth resource list of those agencies. It's an easy way to make a connection with them and encourage their services to students.
- *Speak* at local service groups, such as Lions or AAUW, about libraries and education. (Get permission from your administrators first, citing how the school benefits from this connection.)
- *Train* community members in information skills, youth development, educational technology.
- *Instruct* local youth groups, such as Scouts or 4H.
- *Provide* background research information for a community agency as appropriate, such as reading interests of teens.
- *Seek sponsorship* from local businesses for library events or contests, such as free food coupons as prizes in a reading contest.
- *Display* community work in the library.
- *Host* community speakers in the library.
- *Participate* in local community activities, be it community productions or rec center exercise classes. (And wear your library T-shirt.)
- *Volunteer* to help with a community service project.
- *Join* community interest clubs.

These ties work both ways. You become a more connected member of the community, and you get to know more about the area in which your students live so you can serve them better.

Making Friends with the Media

The community is the media market for local newspapers, broadcast stations, and community bulletin boards. Local media have a responsibility for, as well as an interest in, covering community news. Area cable companies have to maintain a community programming channel in order to be franchised. As you tell the library story to the public, it is imperative that you have an established working relationship with the area's communications channels.

Before sending any message out, check first with your school to see if public relations must be routed through some school official. You need to work in concert with the school, not counter to it. If no such organized structure exists, then you can start it. If you have the time and ability, become that central news-gathering source for the school. It enables you to see what is happening schoolwide and gives you another opportunity for information-based leadership. If an established public relations channel exists, make good use of it to get out the library message more efficiently.

Whether you work with the school's communications officer or directly with the media, introduce yourself to the person in charge. In a larger media company, your best contact might be the education editor. Find out what this person wants in terms of press release content, format, and time frame. What are his deadlines? Does he have particular priorities: human interest stories, time-sensitive news, meaty issues? Does he want regular contributions and contact, or does he prefer as-needed communication? Might he welcome regular columns or essays, which would give the library and you a consistent high profile? See what you can do for the editor. Establish yourself as a good source of news. The more specific the expectations and responsibilities, the greater chance for frequent and effective communications.

You can get out the news in several ways:
- Flyers and posters,
- Press releases,
- Audiocassette and videotape public service announcements,
- Videotape programs on library issues and events,
- Interviews,
- News conferences (supply fact sheets and "sound bites"), and
- Electronic bulletin boards.

In newspapers alone, contributions may take the form of a news story, feature, photo and caption, events listing, summary, column, or letter to the editor. One news item may be the opening to a full-blown feature.

Regardless of the medium or story, a few key points should guide your relations with the media:
- Be truthful, credible, and accurate.
- Be timely and reliable.
- Be professional and knowledgeable.
- Be fair.

Coalition Building

Schools are important components of the community. Let's face it: Our students and teachers spend more time in the community than in school, and the taxpayers keep our doors open. Particularly with the social issues that confront our youth—dysfunctional families, crime, drugs, changing mores—schools realize that they can't do the job alone. They must work with other agencies to provide students a safe and open learning atmosphere.

Coalitions have become a national trend for dealing with limited resources and personnel within any one institution. Coalitions are effective for several reasons:
- They facilitate group action.
- They can pool and share resources.
- They can influence opinion.
- They can form rapidly to deal with pressing issues.
- They can provide common ground for dissimilar interests. (ALA, 1985, p. 18-20)

We school librarians are in a prime position to show leadership in this task. We are natural data-gatherers and organizers. We work collaboratively, sharing information. We are intuitive problem-solvers. We should already have professional contacts with our public library counterparts. Building on that community basis, we can become effective coalition builders and leaders at local, regional, and national levels.

What, then, are the steps to effective coalition building?

- Identify a reason for the coalition to exist; a mutual issue must draw groups together.
- Start with a small group and bring in more people at each step. (This approach simplifies organizational development.)
- Carefully define the coalition's goals and objectives, rules and expectations.
- Negotiate the degree to which groups will agree and to which they will accept each other's differences.
- Educate, coach, and support each group as appropriate.
- Communicate the coalition's actions and credit each member's efforts. (ALA, 1985, p. 25)

Some examples of coalition building include developing strategies to counteract library closings, establishing community homework centers, planning a community-wide career fair, creating a youth center, involving students in community broadcasting, establishing a youth hotline.

Coalitions, though valuable, are not without headaches. They require much negotiating and consensus-building. They demand much time and flexibility. They can feel amorphous and ephemeral. They can be messy. No quick fixes exist, and no guarantees for success. However, coalitions are too important to ignore.

Politics

How much do you know about local politics? Do you know how local government works? Do you know the names of your local officials? Yes, community leadership includes politicking as well. Especially since the local government controls most library and school funding and policy, you need to keep your ear to the ground—and your hands open to help.

Understand that political work for librarians is based on issues, not political parties. In fact, some schools include a nonpartisan clause in their contracts. Rather, as school librarians we need to act as responsible citizens to better our community through appropriate legislation.

As with other community relations, political relations require thoughtful nurturing. Get to know your local government officials—their responsibilities and their priorities. Take time to listen to them and introduce yourself to them in order to develop a personal touch. Respect and make appropriate use of their staff. Educate them about libraries and related issues; become a dependable source of accurate information for them. Get their ear not only during crises, but on a regular basis. And thank them for their support of libraries!

When you lobby, remember these points:

- Legislators respond best to reliable individuals they know personally.
- Give the facts necessary to make an informed decision. Include the opposition's points, and give counter-justifications to prove your point.

- Provide solutions, not just problems. Do background research in order to become current on the topic, both for yourself and for the legislator.
- One person *can* make a difference!

Pro-active work with government, be it local or national, may be an uncomfortable task for you, but you can still support those who enjoy this kind of activity. Acquiring current information on important issues, helping others research pertinent areas of concern, keeping open the market place of ideas in the library—these background efforts enable citizens to practice democracy, which is the foundation for effective library service.

Section 9

Leadership Within the Profession: The Fourth Ring of Power

When a chief is raised up, he is told, "Now you are poorer than any of us. Because you have lost yourself, you have become the nation."

Hazel Dean-Jean, Seneca clan mother

I admit it: I participate actively in professional library organizations. It's because I can learn and share so much. Not only does my service in the school improve, but I become a more effective librarian because of professional connections. It's through these contacts that I have been able to review (and keep) outstanding reference materials, get connected to Internet, improve library instruction, and obtain grants, among other advantages.

I've heard folks say that librarians have more meetings and organizations than most professions. Perhaps so. We have professional ties on several geographic levels, from district to international, as well as by type of library. As school librarians we also connect with educational groups. Perhaps the fact that so many school librarians work with only one or two other staff members pushes us to share mutual interests with librarians and educators in other settings. Regardless of the motivation, though, school librarians have great opportunities to become leaders within the profession. This chapter reveals the secrets of the fourth ring of power: the librarian profession as a whole.

The Challenges

It's all too easy to get nestled into our specific library setting or so wrapped up in fighting daily brush fires that we don't think about librarianship and the challenges of today's society. In the summary report of the 1991 White House Conference on Library and Information Services, several national trends were noted: the explosion of information and technology, problems of growing illiteracy, the need for greater productivity in the face of global competition, and the gap between have's and have-not's in terms of access to information. *Information Power* adds to these problems that of growing and changing diversity.

Librarians are significant players in meeting these challenges. They can help the broadest constituency have access to the "information superhighway." They can ensure access to government information resources. They can work with youth to instill information skills and reading enjoyment. They can facilitate literacy programs. They can be partners in lifelong education. They can enact national information policies for democracy. Librarians are the most viable group to ensure equal access to information for all. (ALA, 1993, p. 14)

Yet the future of libraries and librarians sometimes seems problematic. Witness the number of shortened library hours, lay-offs, and closings of libraries and library schools. Consider the number of school librarians being reduced or replaced by paraprofessionals and volunteers. Too many folks "out there" think that a modem alleviates the need for a librarian. Harsh realities, but true.

Now, although doing our job well in our own little library is lauded, we can advance library service and the profession significantly when we work together with other librarians. And the same skills that enable you to become a leader in other spheres transfer to professional leadership as well.

A Vision of the Profession

In 1991 a group composed mainly of members from the Council of Library Resources met to create a strategic vision for librarianship in the 21st century. Their 1992 draft posited these goals:

- *Service* in providing timely and accurate information with equal access, holding users as central to service and educating them.
- *Leadership* in researching and developing information-related policies, and collaborating with allies in information delivery.
- *Innovation* in developing new forms of organizational structure and staffing for service in various environments, including the "virtual library."
- *Recruitment and development* in attracting and training creative and diverse people and incorporating other disciplines into the field.

For this professional vision to become a reality, we school librarians need to place ourselves in the big picture. We need to commit ourselves to the profession at large.

Networking

The first step in profession-wide leadership is to network with other librarians, both geographically and in relation to type of library. These professional links can be verbal, electronic, or political; they can occur among people, libraries, and organizations; they can be a means for sharing resources, ideas, and policies. By networking, you can share like interests and concerns, test new ideas and projects, learn and teach skills and concepts, coordinate library efforts, and get recognition for your efforts. Particularly as you network across library type and geographic region, you get fresh insights into the field so you can improve service—and yourself.

Organizational membership offers benefits such as:
- Assistance: employment, censorship cases, standards;
- Products: print and nonprint;
- Continuing education: conferences, courses, forums;
- Recognition: scholarships, awards, grants, positions;
- Lobbying: legislation, national issues; and
- Human connections: sharing, support, collaboration.

The easiest way to start is locally with other librarians: within or across district lines, with feeder schools, in consort with public or other types of libraries. These gatherings develop social connections as well as professional expertise, and they enable you to practice leadership skills in a small arena through presentations and joint projects. Your fellow librarians may well have connections with formal library organizations as well, so you can get an idea of what these larger groups do.

Since networking is a two-way street, you will be giving of yourself as well. Take a moment to check ways that you can contribute to networking:

How Can I Contribute?
- Experiential insights: "How I did it good" or "How I wish I'd done it."
- Creative ideas, especially those which you'd like to try but don't have the resources to implement.
- Products: bibliographies, lesson plans, publications, programs.
- Collections: professional reading, specialties, demo programs, audiovisual.
- Facilities: library or other meeting places, catering services.
- Staff: volunteers, speakers and facilitators, teachers.

Networking does have its down side. It takes time and money. You lose some autonomy and control as you negotiate and work with others. And the bureaucratic and political aspects of some professional organizations must be reckoned with. However, the experiences can be long-lasting dividends worth the investment of self. So as you network, choose those groups that most closely meet your needs. Here are some factors to consider:
- What is the group's mission? What are they trying to accomplish?
- What is the group's reputation? What power and influence do they exert?
- What are the benefits of joining? Publications, assistance, status?
- Who are the members? Whom do they represent? What is their level of expertise? What attitudes are prevalent?
- What are the expectations of members? How can members participate? What are the time and financial commitments?

Attend a few meetings, talk with members, look at their literature. If you find like-minded, pro-active professionals with direction, you may have found a potential lifelong support group where you can make a difference while having fun and making friends.

While joining a professional organization helps you keep current with library trends, actively participating in that association enables you to get in-depth professional knowledge, which you can use to improve service at your school and within the broader field.

Attending meetings and conferences allows you to become acquainted with other members as well as learn skills and trends. But such gatherings are just the start. Here are some ways to make headway into the organizational arena:

- Learn about the organization by reading its literature and talking with its members.
- "Adopt" a knowledgeable and active member as a mentor.
- Present papers at conferences.
- Write for organizational publications.
- Join a committee.
- Participate in leadership institutes and other continuing education opportunities.

What organizations appreciate the most are enthusiastic, hard-working, dependable, knowledgeable, personable and involved members. Make your presence and your ideas known, and enthusiastically support the leadership. In return, you will get to see how library leadership *really* works—and you can become a part of that leadership contingent.

Mentoring

As you strive to advance in the profession, just as you strive for leadership within a school setting, you will need help along the way. Certainly you should maintain positive working relationships with your colleagues and superiors, keep abreast of employment opportunities, and participate actively in continuing education activities. But beyond the normal range of professional awareness, you will probably need an extra personal push if you want to move up significantly within the profession.

One of the most typical career stepping stones is mentoring: A more experienced and influential librarian helps pave the career road of a less powerful librarian through sponsorship and individual coaching. The mentor initiates the beginning librarian into the inner professional "club" and paves the way for committee assignments and other forms of power.   The library world is full of examples of such mentor relationships, most of which are informal set-ups. The best way to foster such a situation is to become involved in professional activities and work personably with others.

Career Ladders

Leadership within the field is often correlated with status job positions, although plenty of influential librarians hold small-scale jobs. The basic premise is that as librarians gain knowledge and skills and contribute more to the profession, they are in a better position for career advancement. With more authority comes greater opportunity to network with other leaders in the field, which facilitates inclusion in leader rings of power.

For school librarians, advancement within the system can be difficult, particularly if only one professional staffs the library. Either the librarian looks for a better school library or aspires to a district or multi-site position. The first alternative is considered a lateral move to another faculty staff position; the latter is usually a shift from a faculty to an administrative position. (Only in a few cases are building-level librarians considered administrators.)

Some school librarians wanting career advancement switch to other library settings, usually community or junior college or public libraries. A few go the special library route, join university libraries, or teach at library schools. These transfers usually entail additional training. Interestingly, though, these librarians often retain the function of interacting directly with users, which may not be the case when a site-based librarian becomes a broad-based educational administrator.

Some school librarians may choose to keep a low-profile job so they will have more time to devote to professional organizations. Administrators who understand how professional activities renew and educate their librarians may feel relieved that such a leader chooses to stay secure at the building level. Administrators may also appreciate the name recognition their schools acquire when associated with a professionally recognized leader.

Another factor affecting career patterns can be life style—other priorities besides librarianship, such as family and avocations. Librarians with small children may want to keep in educational circles—as may librarians who enjoy lengthy travel. Librarians who actively publish may prefer part-time work that involves less commitment. Health issues, their own or family members', may also influence librarians' career decisions.

Additionally, librarians may change career paths on a short-term basis. Again, family concerns may postpone a promotion. Time out to pursue an advanced degree or participate in a once-in-a-lifetime opportunity such as a year abroad or a teacher exchange may limit immediate advancement, but certainly help personal and professional growth in the long run.

In short, the routes towards leadership within the library profession are as numerous as the ways to exert librarian leadership. The important factor is conscious, personal choice. How you make good use of whatever position you hold, be it paid or volunteer, be it in a school or within a professional organization, will determine the degree to which you can become an effective leader. Your ring of power may be small, but it can set off larger rings of influence within the profession.

<u>Notes</u>

Section 10
The Audience Role of Following

No matter what accomplishment we make—somebody helps us.
Althea Gibson

In following him I follow but myself.

William Shakespeare

A majority of folktales emphasize the need to follow: "Go straight to Granny's house, and don't talk to the wolf"; "You must find me three . . ."; "Follow the yellow brick road." Heavy penalties resulted from disobedience. Even the hero had to follow certain dictums in order to win freedom or the damsel.

Moreover, when the hero returned triumphant, he needed a cheering crowd. Where would the storyteller be without an audience? So, too, the leader must follow certain paths to attain a goal. And while the leader provides a vision, it takes followers to make the vision a reality.

Particularly in this book, which emphasizes the concept of empowerment and shared power, the role of follower is more important than ever, for the follower is a potential leader. And an effective leader must know how to follow as well. There is, in fact, a kind of ebb and flow of power in highly effective schools. Different persons perform leadership tasks as various needs arise. The result is a highly interdependent and symbiotic atmosphere of mutual support and learning.

So what constitutes a good follower? Obviously, acting professionally is the basis for being a prized employee. Librarians have an ethos of behavior that emphasizes high-quality, courteous service. Within an institution, though, followers have certain responsibilities to their employers:

- To know their job and perform it competently;
- To respect and listen to others;
- To have a cooperative attitude toward accomplishing group goals;
- To support and carry out group decisions; and
- To participate and communicate effectively with the school community.

As a responsible follower, you should act the way you would want others to if *you* were the leader.

Here is a simple exercise to see what kind of follower you value:

- List three people with whom you work very effectively and easily.
- Now list three adjectives that apply to those people.
- Next, list three people with whom you have difficulty working.
- List three adjectives that apply to that group of people.

Analyze the findings to see what patterns and values emerge. How do you fit relative to those two groups of people? What steps can you take to become the follower you want others to be?

Of course, the kind of preferred follower above indicates the type of leader you are. Your own administrator may be a different kind of leader and may be more comfortable with a different style of follower. As a follower, it is your responsibility to discover your leader's preferences and accommodate them while satisfying your own needs.

As a follower you are more than an engaged audience. You assume the role of apprentice. By learning from the experts, you too can be transformed into a leader in your own right when the time comes to prove yourself.

Bibliography

Adams, Linda, and Elinor Lenz. *Effectiveness Training for Women; E.T.W.* New York: Wyden, 1979.

Albano, Charles, and Thomasine Rendero. *Transactional Analysis on the Job & Communicating with Subordinates.* Rev. ed. Washington DC: American Management Association, 1974.

Albritton, Rosie L., and Thomas W. Shaughnesy. *Developing Leadership Skills.* Englewood CO: Libraries Unlimited, 1990.

American Library Association. *Forging Coalitions for the Public Good.* Chicago: ALA, 1985.

American Library Association and Association for Educational Communications and Technology. *Information Power: Guidelines for School Library Media Programs.* Chicago: ALA, 1988.

American Library Association Presidential Committee on Information Literacy. *Final Report.* Chicago: ALA, 1989.

American Library Association President's Committee on Project Century 21. *Project Century 21: A Research and Action Program for Meeting the Information Needs of Society.* Chicago: ALA, 1993.

Anderson, Pauline H. *Library Media Leadership in Academic Secondary Schools.* Hamden CT: Library Professional Publications, 1985.

Bacharach, Samuel B. and Edwin J. Lawler. *Power and Politics in Organizations.* San Francisco: Jossey-Bass, 1981.

Barth, R. *Improving Schools From Within: Teachers, Parents, and Principals Can Make the Difference.* San Francisco: Jossey-Bass, 1990.

Bass, B. M. *Leadership and Performance Beyond Expectations.* New York: Free Press, 1987.

Bennis, Warren, and Burt Nanus. *Leaders: The Strategies for Taking Charge.* New York: Harper-Row, 1985.

Bethel, Sheila Murray. *Making a Difference.* New York: Putnam, 1990.

Bettelheim, Bruno. *Uses of Enchantment.* New York: Vintage, 1977.

Bolman, Lee G., and Terrence E. Deal. *The Path to School Leadership: A Portable Mentor.* Newbury Park CA: Sage, 1993.

Bradford, David, and Allan Cohen. *Influence Without Authority*. New York: Wiley, 1990.

Brandon, Nathaniel. *Six Pillars of Self-Esteem*. New York: Bantam, 1993.

Brock, Susan L., and Sally R. Cabbell. *Writing a Human Resources Manual*. Los Altos: Crisp, 1989.

Brown, Jean. "Leadership for school improvement," *Emergency Librarian* 20:3 (Jan., 1993) 8-20.

Brown, M. T. *Working Ethics*. San Francisco: Jossey-Bass, 1990.

Bryman, Alan. *Leadership and Organizations*. London: Routledge & Kegan Paul, 1986.

Burdenuk, Gene. "Vision and the School Library Resource Center," *Emergency Librarian* 20:3 (Jan., 1993) 22-24.

Burns, J. *Leadership: Multi-Disciplinary Perspectives*. Englewood Cliffs NJ: Prentice-Hall, 1984.

Burns, J. *Leadership*. New York: Harper and Row, 1978.

California Library Association Intellectual Freedom Committee. *Intellectual Freedom Handbook*. Sacramento: CA, 1992.

Campbell, Joseph. *The Hero with a Thousand Faces*. Princeton NJ: Princeton University Press, 1949.

Cawleti, Gordon. *Challenges and Achievements of American Education*. Alexandria VA: Association for Supervision and Curriculum Development, 1993.

Cleaver, Betty P., and William D. Taylor. *Involving the School Library Media Specialist in Curriculum Development*. Chicago: ALA, 1983.

Cohen, William A. *Art of the Leader*. Englewood Cliffs NJ: Prentice Hall, 1990.

Collins, Roger. *Effective Management*. Auckland, New Zealand: Commerce Clearing House, 1993.

Convoy, Barbara, and Barbara Schindler Jones. *Improving Communication in the Library*. Phoenix: Oryx, 1986.

Covey, Stephen R. *Principle-Centered Leadership*. New York: Summit, 1991.

Deal, Terrence E., and A. Kennedy. *Corporate Culture*. Reading MA: Addison-Wesley, 1982.

Dubin, Andrew. *Principal as Chief Executive Officer*. New York: Falmer, 1991.

Duke, D. L. *School Leadership and Instructional Improvement*. New York: Random House, 1987.

Evans, G. Edward. *Management Techniques for Librarians*. New York: Academic Press, 1983.

Educational Leadership (February, 1992). Entire issue devoted to librarian leadership.

Eicholtz, Robert T. "School Climate: Key to Excellence." *American Education* (January, 1984) 22-26.

Elgin, Suzette Daen. *Genderspeak*. New York: Wiley, 1993.

Elster, Jan. *Diversity: Creating Awareness and Avenues*. San Francisco: Bay Area Girl Scout Council, 1993.

Farmer, Lesley. *When Your Library Budget Is Almost Zero*. Englewood Cliffs NJ: Libraries Unlimited, 1993.

Flaxman, Erwin, Carol Ascher and Charles Harrington. *Youth Mentoring: Programs and Practices*. New York: ERIC, 1988.

Galbraith, John Kenneth. *Anatomy of Power*. Boston: Houghton-Mifflin, 1983.

Gardner, John W. *On Leadership*. New York: Free Press, 1990.

Gordon, Thomas. *Leader Effectiveness Training*. New York: Wyden, 1977.

Glickman, Carl. D. *Supervision in Transition*. Alexandria VA: Association for Supervision and Curriculum Development, 1992.

Gorman, Alfred H. *The Leader in the Group*. Teachers College, Columbia University, 1963.

Grahl, Bart, tr. *Cultural Creation in Modern Society*. New York: Telos Press, 1976.

Hartzell, Gary N. "Building Influence for the High School Librarian." *The Book Report* (May 1993) 11-15.

Helgesen, Sally. *Female Advantage: Women's Ways of Leadership.* New York: Doubleday, 1990.

Hellriegel, Don, John W. Slocum, Jr., and Richard W. Woodman. *Organizational Behavior.* 3rd ed. New York: West, 1983.

Heim, Pat. *Hardball for Women.* Chicago: Lowell House, 1992.

Heim, Pat, and Elwood N. Chapman. *Learning to Lead.* Los Altos CA: Crisp, 1990.

Henning, Margaret. *Managerial Woman.* New York: Pocket Book, 1988.

Hersey, Paul, and Kenneth H. Blanchard. *Management of Organizational Behavior: Utilizing Human Resources.* 3rd ed. Englewood Cliffs NJ: Prentice-Hall, 1977.

Hickman, Craig R., and Michael A. Silva. *Creating Excellence: Managing Corporate Culture, Strategy and Change in the New Age.* New York: New American Library, 1984.

Hickman, Craig R. *Mind of a Manager, Soul of a Leader.* New York: Wiley, 1990.

Hitt, William D. *The Leader-Manager.* Columbus OH: Battelle, 1988.

Hord, Shirley M., et al. *Taking Charge of Change.* Alexandria VA: Association for Supervision and Curriculum Development, 1987.

Ivancevich, John M., Andrew D. Szilagyi, Jr., and Marc J. Wallace, Jr. *Organizational Behavior and Performance.* Santa Monica CA: Goodyear, 1977.

Johnson, David W., and Frank P. Johnson. *Joining Together.* Englewood Cliffs NJ: Prentice-Hall, 1975.

Josey, E. J. *Libraries in the Political Process.* Phoenix: Oryx, 1980.

Keirsey, David, and Marilyn Bates. *Please Understand Me: Character and Temperament Types.* Del Mar CA: Prometheus Nemesis, 1978.

Kotler, Philip, and Karen Fox. *Strategic Marketing for Educational Institutions.* Englewood Cliffs NJ: Prentice-Hall, 1985.

Kotter, J. P. *Power and Influence.* New York: Free Press, 1985.

Kouzes, James M., and Barry Z. Posner. *The Leadership Challenge.* San Francisco: Jossey-Bass, 1987.

Krimmelbein, Cindy Jeffrey. *The Choice to Change*. Englewood CO: Libraries Unlimited, 1989.

Kroeger, Otto, and Janet M. Thuessen. *Type Talk: The Sixteen Personality Types That Determine How We Live, Love, and Work*. New York: Delacorte, 1988.

Kulleseid, Eleanor R. *Beyond Survival to Power for School Library Media Professionals*. Hamden CT: Library Professional Publications, 1985.

Levi, Steven C. *Making It!* Palo Alto: Price Stern Sloan, 1990.

Liontos, Lynn Balster. "Transformational Leadership," *Emergency Librarian* (January, 1993) 34-35.

Manz, Charles C., and Henry P. Sims. *Superleadership*. Englewood Cliffs NJ: Prentice-Hall, 1989.

Mathews, Anne J., editor. *Rethinking the Library in the Information Age*. Volume III. Washington, DC: Government Printing Office, 1989.

Nierenberg, Gerard I. *The Art of Negotiating*. New York: Hawthorn, 1968.

Olsen, Karen D. *Mentor Teacher Role: Owner's Manual*. 5th ed. Village of Oak Creek AZ: Books for Educators, 1989.

O'Toole, James. *Vanguard Management*. New York: Doubleday, 1985.

Packer, Arnold H. "Taking Action on the SCANS Report," *Educational Leadership* (March 1992) 27-31.

Patterson, Jerry L. *Leadership for Tomorrow's Schools*. Alexandria VA: Association for Supervision and Curriculum Development, 1992.

Peters, Tom. *Liberation Management*. New York: Knopf, 1992.

Peters, Tom, and Nancy Austin. *Passion for Excellence*. New York: Random House, 1985.

Phillips, Jack J. *Improving Supervisors' Effectiveness*. San Francisco: Jossey-Bass, 1985.

Plachy, Roger. *When I Lead Why Don't They Follow?* Chicago: Bonus, 1986.

Prostano, Emanuel T. and Joyce S. *The School Library Media Center*. 4th ed. Englewood CO: Libraries Unlimited, 1987.

Reed, Sally Gardner. *Saving Your Library*. Jefferson NC: McFarland, 1992.

Riggs, Donald E. and Gordon A. Sabine. *Libraries in the '90s*. Phoenix: Oryx, 1988.

Riggs, Donald E. *Library Communication: The Language of Leadership*. Chicago: ALA, 1991.

Rossie, Charles M., Jr. *Media Resource Guide*. Los Angeles: Foundation for American Communications, 1985.

Rubin, Richard E. *Human Resource Management in Libraries*. New York: Neal-Schuman, 1991.

Schein, E. *Organizational Culture and Leadership*. San Francisco: Jossey-Bass, 1985.

School Library Media Quarterly (Summer, 1987). Leadership issue.

Scott, Cynthia D., and Dennis T. Jaffe. *Empowerment*. Menlo Park CA: Crisp, 1991.

Senge, P. *The Fifth Discipline: The Art and Practice of the Learning Organization*. New York: Doubleday, 1990.

Sergiovanni, Thomas. *Moral Leadership: Getting to the Heart of School Improvement*. San Francisco: Jossey-Bass, 1992.

Sergiovanni, Thomas. *Value-Added Leadership: How To Get Extraordinary Performance in Schools*. Orlando: Harcourt Brace Jovanovich, 1990.

Shakeshaft, C. *Women in Educational Administration*. Newbury Park CA: Sage, 1989.

Sheive, L., and M. Schoenheit. *Leadership: Examining the Elusive*. Alexander VA: Association for Supervision and Curriculum Development, 1987.

Sigband, Norman B. *Communication for Management*. Glenview IL: Scott Foresman, 1969.

Snelbecker, Glenn E. *Learning Theory, Instructional Theory, and Psychoeducational Design*. New York: McGraw-Hill, 1974.

Snyder, K. A., and R. H. Anderson. *Managing Productive Schools: Toward an Ecology*. Orlando: Academic Press, 1986.

Stechert, Kathryn B. "Raising Your Power Consciousness." *Working Woman* (April 1986) 117-120.

Stevens, Norman D. *Communication Throughout Libraries.* Metuchen NJ: Scarecrow, 1983.

Stueart, Robert D., and Barbara B. Moran. *Library Management.* 3rd ed. Littleton CO: Libraries Unlimited, 1987.

Taylor, Pat. "Leadership in Education," *Emergency Librarian* (January 1994) 9-17.

Thompson, Ann McKay, and Marcia Donnan Wood. *Management Strategies for Women.* New York: Simon & Schuster, 1980.

Tichy, N., and M. Devnna. *The Transformational Leader.* New York: Wiley, 1990.

Toffler, Barbara Ley. *Tough Choices: Managers Talk Ethics.* New York: Wiley, 1986.

United States Department of Education. *Alliance for Excellence.* Washington: U. S. Government Printing Office, 1984.

Uris, Auren. *Techniques of Leadership.* McGraw-Hill, 1953.

Walling, Donovan R. *How to Build Staff Involvement in School Management.* Englewood cliffs NJ: Prentice-Hall, 1984.

Wehmeyer, Lillian Biermann. *The School Librarian as Educator.* 2nd ed. Englewood CO: Libraries Unlimited, 1984.

Wilson, Ian. "Realizing the Power of Strategic Vision," *Long Range Planning* (October, 1992) 18-22.

Woolls, Blanche. *Supervision of District Level Library Media Programs.* Englewood CO: Libraries Unlimited, 1990.

Yukl, G. *Leadership in Organizations.* 2nd ed. Englewood Ciffs NJ: Prentice-Hall, 1989.

www.ingramcontent.com/pod-product-compliance
Ingram Content Group UK Ltd.
Pitfield, Milton Keynes, MK11 3LW, UK
UKHW012331270225
455688UK00010B/284